# The Restoration Movement:

## Speaking As the Oracles of God

By L. A. Stauffer

© 2023 Spiritbuilding Publishers.
All rights reserved. No part of this book may be reproduced in any form without the written permission of the publisher.

Published by
Spiritbuilding Publishers
9700 Ferry Road, Waynesville, Ohio 45068

THE RESTORATION MOVEMENT:
Speaking As the Oracles of God
By L.A. Stauffer

ISBN: 978-1955285-79-7

## Spiritbuilding
PUBLISHERS

spiritbuilding.com

## Table of Contents

Chapter 1  Historical Background . . . . . . . . . . . . . . . . . . . . . . . . . . . . . 1

Chapter 2  Early British Movement . . . . . . . . . . . . . . . . . . . . . . . . . . . . 6

Chapter 3  The O'Kelly Secession . . . . . . . . . . . . . . . . . . . . . . . . . . . . . 11

Chapter 4  The New England Movement . . . . . . . . . . . . . . . . . . . . . . . 17

Chapter 5  The Christians: Barton W. Stone . . . . . . . . . . . . . . . . . . . . . 22

Chapter 6  Declaration and Address: Thomas Campbell . . . . . . . . . . . . . . 32

Chapter 7  A Restoration of the Ancient Order: Alexander Campbell . . . . 41

Chapter 8  The New Evangelism: Walter Scott . . . . . . . . . . . . . . . . . . . . 54

Chapter 9  The Merging of the Two Groups . . . . . . . . . . . . . . . . . . . . . 64

Chapter 10  Innovations and Change . . . . . . . . . . . . . . . . . . . . . . . . . . . 72

Chapter 11  A Slogan: Its Test and Meaning . . . . . . . . . . . . . . . . . . . . . . 82

Chapter 12  Division: Three Separate Groups . . . . . . . . . . . . . . . . . . . . . 95

Chapter 13  Church of Christ: A History of New Controversies . . . . . . . . . 109

*Publisher's Note* . . . . . . . . . . . . . . . . . . . . . . . . . . . . . . . . . . . . . . . . . 121

**Appendix 1:** Aftermath of the Institutional Controversy . . . . . . . . . . . . 122

**Appendix 2:** The Post-Modernist Express into the 21st Century . . . . . . 137

## Chapter 1
# Historical Background
## Introduction

Jesus promised and built His church in the first century (Matthew 16:18; Ephesians 1:22–23), which is the body of obedient believers over which He alone rules as head. Before the close of the New Testament, the Spirit warned that an apostasy would occur (Acts 20:29–30; 1 Timothy 4:1–3), where brethren would speak perverse things, draw away disciples after them, and depart from the faith. That apostasy, including the rise of Catholicism and Protestant denominationalism, provides the historical background that both demanded and provoked the Restoration Movement.

A brief look at that background is the subject of our first lesson.

## Catholicism: An Apostate Perversion of Christianity

**Bishop/Pope**

The apostasy showed its first signs in the distinction made early in the second century between bishops and presbyters. Over a period of centuries bishops gave rise to metropolitans in capital cities of Roman provinces, then to patriarchs in the chief cities of the empire, and finally a universal bishop, the pope of Rome. All of this was accomplished by 606 A.D.

**Clergy/Sacraments**

During those same centuries, bishops and presbyters were exalted to the status of a special priesthood by which access to grace was possible only by their administration of what came to be called sacraments. The sacraments were systematized and set in place by the time of Thomas Aquinas (A.D. 1225?–1274).

**Mass/Mystery**

Alongside the organizational apostasy developed a mystical view of the Lord's Supper in which the elements of bread and fruit of the vine were viewed as containing the actual body and blood of Jesus. This perversion began as early as Justin Martyr (150 A.D.) and was fully defined in the doctrine of transubstantiation at the Council of Trent (1540s A.D.).

## Baptism/Sprinkling

Mainly in cases of sickness or other demands of convenience the original practice of immersion for baptism was shortened to pouring water on a candidate and finally to the present practice of sprinkling. This began in cases of emergency as early as the third century.

## Penance/Indulgences

Out of all this perversion the straw that broke the camel's back, along with priestly immorality and corruption, and provoked the Reformation Movement was the sale of indulgences in connection with the sacrament of penance. This amounted to the sale of relief from purgatorial suffering and, in some cases, the actual forgiveness of sins.

# Protestantism: A Proliferation of Denominational Division

## *Luther; Zwingli/Calvin; Henry VIII; Conrad Grebel*

Fundamentally, four wings of the reformation of Catholicism developed over the early decades of the 1500s.

### Lutheran

Out of the original work of Martin Luther in Germany came the various sects of the Lutheran church and the Moravian brethren.

### Reformed

Out of the work of Ulrich Zwingli and John Calvin in Switzerland developed the various "Reformed" churches and the variety of Presbyterians.

### Anglican

Out of the revolt of Henry VIII against the authority of the pope arose the Church of England or what is sometimes called the Anglican church. From the movement also came the Protestant Episcopal church, Methodist church, Wesleyan churches, Nazarene, Quakers, Puritans, and Congregationalists which later aligned themselves with the Reformed churches.

### Anabaptist

Conrad Grebel questioned infant baptism and started the Anabaptist (baptism again) movement which spawned the Mennonites, Amish, and various Baptist churches.

## *Principles, Flaws, and Results*

The chief ideas or principles of the Reformation Movement were:

1. The authority of the Scriptures
2. The priesthood of all believers
3. Salvation by faith alone

By these principles they fought the authority of the pope, the corruption and role of the priesthood, and the earning of salvation by the works of penance. The fatal flaw of reformation theology was the concept of salvation by "faith only." This rendered unimportant and unnecessary any aspect of Christianity but trust in Christ for salvation by grace.

The result of "faith only" salvation guaranteed the proliferation of religious denominationalism into a thousand divisive bodies. Those quickly arose where political freedom supported their rights to separateness, especially in the new world, the Americas.

# Restoration: A Search for the Ancient Order

Men bent on restoration saw the divisions of denominationalism as contrary to Jesus' prayer for unity in John 17:20–21. They also believed denominationalism contradicted the teachings of the apostles in 1 Corinthians 1:10–13 and Ephesians 4:1–6. Those championing the Restoration Movement pursued as a plan for unity the restoring of the ancient order and practices of the primitive church. This unity, they argued, calls, first, for the elimination of all human creeds and traditions of men. Their effort gave birth to the plea and motto: "Let us speak where the Scriptures speak and be silent where the Scriptures are silent" (Thomas Campbell).

Some of the men who moved in this direction that we will study in some detail included: John Glas, Robert Sandeman, Robert and James Haldane, Elias Smith, Abner Jones, Barton W. Stone, Thomas and Alexander Campbell, and Walter Scott.

Luke 8:11 and Matthew 13:19 speak of the word of God as the seed of the kingdom. Since every seed produces after its own kind it was believed if the word of God, the seed, was sown into good and honest hearts, the kingdom or church of the first century could be reproduced in the 19th, 20th or any other century.

## Conclusion

When men of the Restoration Movement went back to the Bible and saw the error of "faith only," they found that several matters beyond faith must characterize the people of God. They saw the importance of terms of entrance into the church, also the significance of the name, the organization, the work, and the worship of the church.

## Discussion

1. What did Jesus promise to build? Where is this recorded? Who is the head of the church? How do you know? Men would arise and speak what? What would they do with disciples? They would depart or fall away from what?

2. What initial change ultimately led to the pope of Rome? Bishops and presbyters became a special what? What did they administer? What happened to the Lord's Supper? What did baptism become? Why? What principally led to the Reformation?

3. Who were the four main men of the Reformation? What groups came out of Luther's work? Zwingli/Calvin? Henry VIII? Conrad Grebel? What were the chief ideas of the Reformation? What was the fatal flaw? What resulted?

4. What Biblical idea does denominationalism violate? What did men of the Restoration pursue to bring about unity? What did they believe must be eliminated? What was their motto? What Biblical principle justifies restoration?

5. What did men of the Restoration consider important beyond "faith only?"

## Chapter 2

# Early British Movements

## Introduction

Although the concept of restoring the primitive church was not unknown to the Reformation era (1500s), the American 19th century restoration had a sounder basis and made a more lasting impression. Its earliest roots are found among British preachers and theologians.

Before they came to America both Thomas and Alexander Campbell, significant American restorationists, had opportunity to hear and assess the ideas of these British preachers. These ideas were also brought by others to America where they touched the life of Walter Scott, an associate of the Campbells.

The men of Britain associated with the restoration idea were not as equally devoted to the unity of all religious bodies through this return to first-century Christianity. The idea of unity was not a significant point of emphasis with them.

This lesson looks at the principal men of Britain who were devoted to restoring the primitive church: John Glas, Robert Sandeman, Robert and James Haldane, and Greville Ewing.

## John Glas and Robert Sandeman

### *John Glas*

John Glas was born in 1695 and died in 1773. He was a Presbyterian minister in the church of Scotland until 1728, "when he adopted independent views and formed churches in most of the large towns in Scotland."[1] "Glas withdrew from the church of Scotland primary because he had become convinced it was wrong in having a connection with the state and in having synods and other religious law-making bodies to fix standards of doctrine for the whole church and exercise discipline over it, whereas the New Testament church had none of these things."[2]

---

1 *Journey in Faith*, Lester G. McAllister and William E. Tucker, p. 94.
2 *The Disciples of Christ: A History*, Winfred Earnest Garrison and Alfred T. DeGroot, p. 47.

"His great concern was with the procedure by which the autonomous local congregation should order its affairs, conduct its public worship, establish its ministry, and discipline its members, all in strict accordance with the practice of the apostolic churches depicted in the New Testament".[3] Glas believed the Lord's Supper ought to be observed more frequently than annually or monthly, "as the first disciples came together on the first day of the week for breaking bread"; they ought "to be followers of the first churches, being guided and directed by the Scriptures alone." "They found in every one of them (primitive churches) there was a plurality of elders."[4]

## *Robert Sandeman*

Robert Sandeman was the son-in-law of John Glas. He was born in 1718 and died in 1771. He was a "theological thinker and writer of great power. His works were widely read and highly regarded by many."[5]

"Robert Sandeman was a much more striking character than Glas, and the development of his thought offered an additional parallel to one point which was prominent in the position of Mr. Campbell and the Disciples of Christ. Sandeman argued that saving faith is simply an act of man's mind by which he believes testimony concerning Jesus Christ."[6] This was a significant departure from Calvinism, a fundamental view of Alexander Campbell, and a point of much contention with the Baptists.

"He afterward went to America, founded a congregation at Danbury, Connecticut, in 1763, and remained there the rest of his life. This congregation affiliated with the Disciples shortly after 1840. There were probably never more than twenty to thirty churches of this order in Great Britain or America."[7] These groups were often known as "Glasites," "Sandemanians" or "Old Scotch Independents."

The chief importance of these men was their stress upon restoring the practice of the primitive church, an emphasis found in the Campbells' writings and in other American movements. The idea of reproducing the New Testament church, including the weekly Lord's Supper, a plurality of elders in each church, and faith based on testimony, was long circulated in Great Britain by these men and others before Thomas and Alexander Campbell were born in Scotland, moved to Ireland, and came to America.

---

3    *Ibid.*, p. 47.
4    *Memoir of John Glas,* xii, quoted by Garrison/DeGroot, p. 47.
5    Garrison/DeGroot, *Disciples...*, p. 48.
6    *Ibid.*, p. 48.
7    McAllister/Tucker, *Journey...*, p. 94.

"The outstanding difference was the total absence of the unity motive in Sandeman and its primacy with Campbell. The Sandeman churches were completely preoccupied with the duty of restoring practices of the primitive church. They had no interest in unity, and not enough evangelistic zeal to keep themselves alive."[8]

## Robert and James Haldane

The Haldane brothers were wealthy members of the Church of Scotland. Robert lived from 1764 to 1842 and James was born in 1768 and died in 1851. They were "disgusted by the formalism and sterility of the established church"[9] and "spent their money freely in promoting an evangelistic revival in Scotland and in building tabernacles in Edinburgh and Glasgow."[10] The Haldanes invited Rowland Hill, a famous evangelist of the time, to hold meetings in Scotland. They also built a tabernacle in Edinburgh to serve as the center for this work.

This is significant because of the connection that Rowland Hill had at Rich Hill, the home of Thomas Campbell. More on this later. Hill never left the church of England, of which he was a deacon, but the Haldanes "could not find scope in their activities with the old church. ...In 1799 they withdrew from the Church of Scotland and organized an independent church in Edinburgh." James Haldane, at age 31, became the church's minister and continued in the capacity for 51 years.

"On the recommendation of Mr. Greville Ewing, a former Church of Scotland minister who was in charge of the Haldane's seminary in Glasgow, they adopted congregational independence as being the order of the New Testament churches and introduced the weekly observances of the Lord's Supper for the same reason." The name Ewing must be remembered for his relationship to Alexander Campbell at the University of Glasgow in 1808.

After the beginning of the 19th century the Haldanes "moved rapidly toward a fuller expression of the conviction that any reformation of the church required exact conformity to the apostolic teaching and practice." In 1805 J. A. Haldane published a volume the full title of which exhibits this conviction fully developed: *A View of the Social Worship and Ordinances Observed by the First Christians, drawn from the Scriptures Alone; Being an Attempt to Enforce Their Divine Obligation; and to Represent the Guilty and Evil Consequences of*

---

8   Garrison/DeGroot, *Disciples...*, p. 50.
9   *Ibid.*, p. 50.
10  McAllister/Tucker, *Journey...*, p. 95.

*Neglecting Them*. Note the emphasis on the first century practice and the authority of the Scriptures.

"This book deals especially with church organization and offices, ordinances, discipline, and the elements which enter into public worship." The first couple of chapters show the direction and emphasis of Haldane's search. Chapter one: "There is reason to presume that the New Testament furnishes instruction concerning every part of the worship and conduct of Christian societies, as well as concerning the faith and practices of individuals." Chapter two: "All Christians are bound to observe the universal and approved practices of the first churches recorded in the scriptures."[11]

They, at first, defended sprinkling by example of circumcision and the 'everlasting covenant,' but, "in 1807 the Haldanes became convinced that the scriptural form of baptism was immersion and abandoned the practice of baptizing infants."[12] "Several other Haldanean churches were established in Scotland and a few in America. It is impossible to say how many because they did not call themselves by that name."[13]

The importance and relationship of these men to our study are seen in their ideas of "restoration" and "scriptural authority" and their contact with the Campbells and Walter Scott.

## Conclusion

Out of the work of these men came the idea of restoration, congregational independence, weekly observance of the Lord's Supper, authority of the scriptures alone, baptism by immersion, plurality of elders in each congregation, and faith by the evidence of testimony. All these gain emphasis in various American movements toward restoration.

The influence of these men who came to America is not fully known, but what is known is that both Thomas and Alexander Campbell had access to many of these ideas before they came from Ireland to America. Also, that Walter Scott had contact with an "Old Scotch Independent" church in New York and worshiped with a "Haldanean" group in Pittsburgh. More on this when we study these men in detail.

---

11   This and the above quotes on this page are from Garrison/DeGroot, *Disciples…*, p. 51–52.
12   McAllister/Tucker, p. 96.
13   Garrison/DeGroot, p. 52.

# Discussion

1. Where does the American restoration find its roots? What three American men were influenced by British preachers? What idea of the American restoration did British theologians not emphasize?

2. What are the dates of John Glas? What church was he associated with? Why did he leave the church of Scotland? What was his greatest concern? List several basic views he held.

3. How was Sandeman related to Glas? What were his dates? How does faith come according to him? When did he come to America? What did he do in 1763? What was the chief importance of Glas and Sandeman's work? List several pre-Campbell ideas. What did Sandeman and Glas think of Presbyterian baptism?

4. What were the dates of each brother? What disgusted them the most? What famous evangelist did they support? When did these two men leave the church of Scotland? Who ran their seminary? Who had a connection with Ewing? What idea is emphasized in the first two chapters of J. A. Haldane's book? What did they learn about baptism in 1807?

# Chapter 3

# The O'Kelly Secession

## Introduction

The earliest movement on American soil to return to primitive ideas of the New Testament church occurred within the ranks of the Methodist Episcopal Church. The movement is often called among Methodists as "The O'Kelly Secession," since its principal leader was Thomas O'Kelly of North Carolina who seceded from the Methodist Church.

"The specific issue which brought about the rupture was the question of episcopacy verses congregational polity, but this question led ultimately to larger issues of biblical interpretation and doctrine."[14]

In this lesson we will look briefly at the background of Methodism in America, the controversy that arose over organization, and the results of the O'Kelly secession.

## Background: The Methodist Church in America

As early as 1729 the leaven of freedom and greater spirituality began working in the Church of England "when John Wesley, noting the formality and tyranny of the Church, proposed forming societies within the church dedicated to the purifying of corrupt elements."[15] These societies, which demanded a holier life among the members of the Church of England, were formed throughout the colonies of America.

"The common belief of apostolic succession prevailed among Anglican clergymen in those days" and no preacher could be ordained except by an official minister of the Church of England, whose ordination allegedly is traceable to the apostles. "The Anglican clergymen who were ordained refused to ordain these preachers of the Wesleyan societies."[16].

"The whole matter then, become one of grave concern, for in time, the distinct existence of the Wesleyan Societies within the Anglican Church was threatened. The question of what could be done in such a crisis was raised on

---

14  *Journey of Faith,* Lester G. McAllister and William E. Tucker, p. 53.
15  *The Search for the Ancient Order,* Earl Irvin West, p. 3.
16  Ibid., p. 5.

both sides of the Atlantic, and considerable anxiety prevailed".[17]

By the end of the Revolutionary War the Anglican clergymen, who has cast their lot with the Tories, had fled to England, leaving the societies and their preachers, who were crying for liberty, as desolate sheep without any ordained leader. On September 2, 1784, John Wesley ordained Thomas Coke as the superintendent in America and Richard Whatcoat and Thomas Vasey as presbyters to be sent with Coke to America. They arrived November 3. Coke's work, as authorized by Wesley, was to set the societies in order.

Coke had plans to constitute the societies as an "Episcopal" church by using his "powers of ordination to make" Francis Asbury a superintendent." At the famous Christmas Conference in Baltimore in 1784, Asbury was ordained as Superintendent of the church in America. It was at this conference that the discipline for the Methodist Episcopal Church was accepted, and here, too, for the first time, the title, Methodist Episcopal Church, was accepted as the name for the Wesleyan Societies".[18]

Asbury promptly changed his title to "bishop" and proceeded to exercise ecclesiastical powers with a strong hand. "Among other things, he assigned every presiding elder to his district, every preacher to his circuit, and from his decision there was no appeal."[19] This soon became a source of controversy among some of the preachers and elders.

"Scarcely had the Methodist Church started, until its first serious internal conflict began to rage. The cause was over a disagreement as to the type of government chosen for the church. There were those who looked upon this government as contrary to the Scriptures … its interest to us lies in the fact that it presents the first major attempt of any people to go back to New Testament Christianity."[20]

## Controversy: The O'Kelly Secession

James O'Kelly (sometimes spelled O'Kelley) was probably born in 1735. He died October 16, 1826, at the age of 92. "O'Kelly had become a Methodist lay preacher in 1775."[21] "He was active and efficient in the shock troops

---

17   Ibid., p. 5.
18   Ibid., p. 6.
19   McAllister/Tucker, p. 53–54.
20   West, p. 6.
21   McAllister and Tucker say he started preaching in 1778.

(nicknamed "Asbury's Ironsides"), which led the early Methodist advance in Maryland, Virginia, and North Carolina."[22]

"O'Kelly loved John Wesley, who having never seen he trusted as an interpreter of the Scriptures. It impressed him that Wesley honored only the Scriptures as authoritative in matters religious."[23] The societies ministers, he said, "come unto us under the direction of John Wesley, whose name to me is of precious memory. His writings magnified the Bible and gave it preference and honor; he declared he regarded the authority of no writings but the inspired. He urged the sufficiency of the Scriptures for the faith and practice saying, "We will be downright Bible Christians.'"[24]

"The influence of Francis Asbury was everywhere seen, and in southern Virginia and North Carolina where O'Kelly traveled, the general impression was that Asbury was a religious tyrant. Fires of opposition were smoldering. His rule was to 'pay, pray, and obey....'. For several years O'Kelly "found himself at odds with Asbury continually. By the time of the famous Christmas Conference in Baltimore, O'Kelly was generally recognized as against Asbury's views."[25] At this conference O'Kelly was ordained a preacher and then: "A week after this conference O'Kelly and twelve others were ordained elders by Thomas Coke. Returning from the conference, O'Kelly began to round up his forces for a show down battle with Asbury."[26]

"As early as 1790 O'Kelly raised questions as to the propriety of having bishops and led a minority of preachers in a futile protest over Asbury's assumption of episcopal powers. Asbury made O'Kelly a presiding elder, but, even then, what seemed to them as an unscriptural assertion of authority."[27]

"At the Methodist General Conference in 1792 O'Kelly introduced a resolution permitting a preacher the right to appeal to the conference if he did not like the appointment he received from the bishop. After three days of heated debate, the resolution was voted down. Thereupon O'Kelly and several other preachers withdrew from the conference. The break in the Methodist ranks is commonly referred to as the "O'Kelly Secession'".[28]

---

22  Garrison/DeGroot, p. 85.
23  *The Stone-Campbell Movement,* Leroy Garret, p. 73.
24  West, p. 7–8.
25  Ibid., p. 8.
26  Ibid., p. 9.
27  McAllister/Tucker, p. 54.
28  Ibid., p. 54–55.

Only O'Kelly and Rice Haggard continued opposition to Asbury. At Piney Grove in Chesterfield County, Virginia, on August 2, 1793, "They petitioned Asbury to meet them in a conference to examine the government of the Methodist Episcopal Church by the scriptures. Asbury refused to meet."[29] "The following December those who had seceded decided to sever all relations with the Methodist Episcopal Church and to take the name Republican Methodists. They were said to have had, at this time, fewer than 1000 members."[30]

## Results: The Christian Church

"The next general meeting of the O'Kelly group was perhaps its most important. The meeting was held August 4, 1794, at Old Lebanon in Surry County, Virginia. The committee of seven had been appointed to devise a plan of church government. Finally, they decided to lay aside every manuscript and go by the Bible alone."[31]

Rice Haggard stood before the group and made the following significant statement about the Bible: "Brethren, this is a sufficient rule of faith and practice. By it we are told that the disciples were called Christians, and I move that henceforth and forever the followers of Christ be known as Christians simply".[32]

They, after the suggestion that they follow the Bible alone, devised what were called the *Five Cardinal Principles of the Christian Church*. West summarizes them as follows:

1. The Lord Jesus as the only Head of the Church.
2. The name Christian to the exclusion of all party and sectarian names.
3. The Holy Bible, or the Scriptures of the Old and New Testament as our only creed, and a sufficient rule of faith and practice.
4. Christian character, or vital piety, the only test of church fellowship and membership.
5. The right of private judgment, and the liberty of conscience in the privilege and duty of all.[33]

It was not until 1801 that the "Republican Methodists" changed their name to the Christian church.

---

29   West, p. 9.
30   McAllister/Tucker, p. 55.
31   West, p. 10.
32   *Ibid.*, p. 10.
33   *Ibid.*, p. 10.

West makes this important observation: "The significance of O'Kelly's action lies in the main, in the direction he was looking. Theirs was a movement to overthrow human elements in religion and go only by the scriptures. That weaknesses appear in their five cardinal principles is evident, but that they were on the high road back to the ancient order is equally evident".[34]

## Conclusion

The O'Kelly Secession is important also because of O'Kelly's connection with Rice Haggard who also had a connection with Barton W. Stone, whom we will consider in a later lesson. Haggard's thinking seems to have reached farther back toward the primitive pattern than did O'Kelly's. In 1804 he wrote a document entitled: *An Address to the Different Religious Societies on the Sacred Import of the Christian Name.* In his pamphlet, Haggard exalts the name of Christ and sets forth a plan for unity.

"The way of unity is in fact," Haggard contended, "for all parties to discard their sectarian name and to wear the name that God gave to His church."[35]

Haggard then presented his plan for unity, consisting of eight points:

1. We are to worship one God…
2. Acknowledge one Savior, Jesus Christ…
3. Let the Bible be the one and only confession of faith.
4. Let us have one form of discipline and government, and let this be the New Testament, which is the constitution of the New Testament Church.
5. Let all Christians consider themselves members of one another.
6. All Christians ought to be members of one church … and the name of this body originates from its head, which makes it "the Christian Church," or the "Church of Christ."
7. Let all profess one religion…
8. Let none be received as members of the church but such as are made alive in Christ.[36]

Churches influenced by O'Kelly became either part of the Stone movement or the New England movement, subjects of our study in the next two lessons. Those connected with the New England movement took a different route from the Restoration movement and were ultimately aligned with "Christian groups in Ohio and Indiana to form the Christian Convention

---

34  *Ibid.*, p. 10.
35  Garrett, p. 86
36  *Ibid.*, p. 86.

in the United States. This church united with the Congregational Church to become the Congregational Christian Churches in 1931."[37]

## Discussion

1. Where did the earliest movement of restoration on American soil begin? What name was given to it? What provoked the movement?

2. What provoked the rise of the societies in the Church of England? Who was behind the societies? What did the societies lack in America? Who did Wesley ordain in 1784 to solve this problem? Who did Coke make superintendent? To what did Asbury change his title? What authority did Asbury have?

3. Who had a problem with Methodist bishops? Why did O'Kelly like Wesley so well? How did O'Kelly view Asbury? To what was O'Kelly ordained by Coke? What did O'Kelly seek to do in 1792? What was the result? What did O'Kelly and Rice Haggard form?

4. What did Haggard state before the group that met in August of 1794? What are the five cardinal principles devised by O'Kelly and Haggard? When did the official adopt the name "Christian?"

5. What connection does Haggard have to a lasting element in the Restoration movement? In 1804 Haggard contended that the way to unity demanded what? List the ideas Haggard stressed in his address of 1804.

---

37  McAllister/Tucker, p. 55.

# Chapter 4

# The New England Movement

## Introduction

The New England movement developed from the independent reactions of two young men against Calvinistic doctrines which prevailed in the Baptist churches of which they were members and for which they were beginning to preach, as well as in the Congregational and Presbyterian churches of the time."[38]

Elias Smith and Abner Jones, the two men referred to above, provided little permanent support to the restoration idea and movement, but do illustrate the climate of inquiry, independence, and pursuit of New Testament ideas that prevailed among many in America at the turn of the 19th century.

A look at the New England movement provides insight into three or four major ideas that surfaced here and several places within the Protestant denominational bodies of the late 1700s and early 1800s. Let's look briefly at these two men, their lives, and their ideas.

## Elias Smith

Smith was born on June 17, 1769, at Lyme, Connecticut in New London County. His father Stephen, "was a Baptist until just one year before his death when a church was formed at Woodstock, Vermont which was 'called by the ancient name recorded in Acts 11:26, Christians.'"[39] Wearing the name "Christian" was one of the major ideas accepted by Smith and commonly advocated in the early 1800s. More on this later.

By May of 1779, just before his tenth birthday, Smith came to believe that believers were the only people to be baptized, and that immersion was the proper method." Later he "became a member of the Second Baptist Church in Woodstock, Connecticut". It was another ten years before Smith "began thinking of becoming a preacher ... He began therefore, an intensive study of the Bible".[40] The more he studied and the more he preached among the Baptists—the more agitated he became with their Calvinistic views of election.

---

38  Garrison/DeGroot, p. 87.
39  West, p. 11.
40  *Ibid.*, p. 12–13.

In the fall of 1801 Smith moved to Salisbury, New Hampshire. "As he studied the New Testament ... he became more and more dissatisfied with orthodox Calvinism and moved toward the conviction not only that this particular system was wrong but that the whole idea of standardized bodies of doctrine and creeds as tests of fellowship was wrong."[41]

"In the spring of 1802, having rejected Calvinism and universalism to search the scriptures to find the truth, I found the name which the followers of Christ ought to wear, which was *Christians* (Acts 11:26). My mind being fixed upon this as the right name, to the exclusion of all the popular names in this world, in the month of May, at a man's house in Epping, N. H., by the name of Laurence, I ventured for the first time, softly to tell people that the name, *Christian,* was enough for the followers of Christ without the addition of the words, *Baptists, Methodists,* etc."[42]

Note both the emphasis on scripture as the basis of truth and the exclusiveness of the name Christian. "At this same meeting," West notes, "Smith spoke against the catechism as being 'an invention of men'."[43]

"At Portsmouth, New Hampshire, in October 1802, the friends of Elias Smith rented a hall called "Jefferson Hall" over the market and began holding regular meetings here every Sunday morning. Arrangements were made for Smith and his family to move there, which they did early the following December". Smith himself wrote, "When our number was some short of twenty, we agreed to consider ourselves a church of Christ, owning him as our only Master, Lord, and Lawgiver, and we agreed to consider ourselves Christians, without the addition of any unscriptural name."[44]

In 1803 the brethren "had been meeting to draw up church articles. The meeting they referred to as a 'Christian Conference.' But, in 1805, when this Conference met, it was agreed that their activities were useless and so they abandoned them, taking the New Testament as the 'only and all-sufficient rule for the Christians'."[45]

## Abner Jones

Abner Jones was born at Royalton, Massachusetts, on April 28, 1772. "Until he was twenty years old, he lived an irreligious and reckless life. In the spring

---

41   Garrison/DeGroot, p. 88.
42   West, p. 13.
43   *Ibid.*, p. 13.
44   *Ibid.*, p. 14.
45   *Ibid.* p. 13–14.

of 1793, he was converted and baptized into the Baptist church by Elder Elisha Ransom, a Baptist preacher.[46] "While still in his early twenties he broke with the Calvinistic Baptists after hearing a sermon by Elias Smith, though Smith at the time was still in the fellowship with the Baptists."[47]

After his dissent from Calvinism, "the Baptist church gave him the cold shoulder. He became more determined than ever to study the Bible and preach just want it taught."[48] "It was in the fall of 1801 that he organized this 'free church' in Lyndon, Vermont, which rejected human names, members insisting solely upon the name *Christian*. In 1802 he organized churches in Hanover and Piermont, New Hampshire".[49]

After 1802, Jones' life and work is intertwined with Elias Smith in establishing churches throughout New England. "Smith was now persuaded to break his Baptist tie, and he was joined by Jones in organizing a Christian church at Portsmouth, New Hampshire. Jones moved to Boston and formed a church there in 1804, and a little later, one in Salem, where he lived for several years."[50]

## The Results of Their Work

A correspondent in the *Advocate and Messenger* in 1827 reported in his travels across New England that he had found "nearly 100 companies of free brethren that met together to worship God in the name of Christ without the addition of any other name".[51] "The Christian churches deriving from the original impulse given by Abner Jones and Elias Smith spread throughout New England and into Canada, New York, New Jersey, Pennsylvania, and northern Ohio".[52]

Their beliefs and practices were described in this way: "We mean to be New Testament Christians, without any sectarian name connected with it, without any sectarian creeds, articles, or confessions, or discipline to illuminate the Scriptures. It is our design to remain free from all human laws, confederations, and unscriptural combinations and to stand fast in the liberty wherewith Christ has made us free".[53]

---

46   Ibid., p. 16.
47   Garrison/DeGroot, p. 89.
48   West, p. 17.
49   Ibid., p. 17.
50   Garrison/DeGroot, p. 89.
51   Ibid., p. 90.
52   Ibid., p. 91–92.
53   Ibid., p. 90.

# Conclusion

"This New England movement, as we have said, owes its primary significance to the fact that men and women were looking in the direction of the New Testament order of things, and away from sectarianism."[54] These men and groups gave little emphasis to the unity of all Christians, but did look to the Scriptures as sole authority, to restoring the divine name, to independence of congregations, and to freedom from bondage to human traditions.

They did not go as far as the Campbells and Stone in restoring first-century Christianity and, as a result, developed little association and affiliation with mainstream congregations of the restoration movement.

# Discussion

1. How did the New England movement begin? Who were the principal men who had a part in it? What do these men illustrate about the climate of the times?

2. When and where was Elias Smith born? What was a major point with Smith? When and how old was Smith when he was baptized? What did he believe about baptism? What church was he associated with? When did he begin to think about preaching? What did he decide to do? What agitated him? Where did he move to in 1801? What besides Calvinism did he oppose? What did he learn by 1802 and begin to whisper softly? What else did he emphasize? What did he speak against? What did the group he met with consider themselves? By 1805 what did the group accept as a rule?

---

54  West, p. 17.

3. Where and when was Abner Jones born? What kind of life did he live as a teenager? What happened in the spring of 1793? Who did he hear preach and what did he do shortly after his baptism? What did he determine after being shunned by the Baptists? What did he do in the fall of 1801? In 1802? What did he reject? What did he insist on? What did he and Smith do after 1802? Where are some of the places they established churches?

4. How plentiful were these groups in New England? Where else did they establish churches? List some of their beliefs and practices.

5. What is the primary significance of the New England movement? What did they give little emphasis to? What were their main emphases? What is their relationship to Campbell and Stone?

# Chapter 5

# The Christians: Barton W. Stone

## Introduction

The Great Revival (1800–1860), a phase of the Second Awakening in America, was to sow the seed that led Barton W. Stone into the Presbyterian Church and from a career in law to a commitment to preach Christ. Stone's study of the Bible created problems in his mind with Calvinism and the teachings of the Westminster Confession of Faith. This gradually drew him away from the Presbyterian Church into a plea for the unity of all believers in one body.

By 1832, Stone's efforts, along with many fellow workers, had converted, by some estimates, 10,000 people who began to unify with disciples converted by the Campbells to form one movement to restore "the ancient order of things." Barton W. Stone, a student of the classics, was a capable writer and left to the Restoration movement three memorable literary works:

- *The Apology of the Springfield Presbytery.*
- *The Last Will and Testament of the Springfield Presbytery.*
- *The Christian Messenger.*

A survey of the life and work of Stone is essential to a complete understanding of the Restoration movement and its growth in American society.

## Barton W. Stone: Student Who Becomes Presbyterian Preacher

"December 24, 1792, Mary Warren Musgrave Stone, wife of John Stone, became the mother of a son she named Barton Warren, in honor of her father."[55] Stone was born at Port Tobacco, Maryland. By 1790 the family was living in Pittsylvania County, Virginia, some thirty miles northeast of Guilford Academy—a prestigious school conducted by David Caldwell near Greensboro, North Carolina. At this academy that year Stone began his

---

55   West, p.18.

pursuit of a law degree by studying the "classics," a course he completed in just three years.

David Caldwell "was a graduate of the College of New Jersey (now Princeton) and a Presbyterian minister of the New Light type. He had come to North Carolina as a pioneer preacher."[56] Caldwell's academy "had a warmly religious atmosphere and was hospitable to the revivalism of the Methodists, Baptists, and "New Light" Presbyterians."[57] James McGready, a prominent Presbyterian preacher and "the chief initiator of the Great Western Revival, had preached near the present Greensboro and converted most of the students in Caldwell's school just before Stone arrived".[58]

McGready returned when Stone was at the academy and his "message was enthusiastic and powerful and Stone himself wrote of its effects: 'For one year I was tossed on the waves of uncertainty—laboring, praying, and striving to obtain saving faith—sometimes desponding, and all-most despairing, of ever getting it".[59] McGready's hellfire, brimstone doom of the non-elect and his view that sinners must wait for the miracle of salvation in God's own time did not sit well with Stone.

"Amidst this anxiety, Stone went in the spring of 1791 to Alamance and heard William Hodge of Hawfields, North Carolina."[60] Here the atmosphere and approach was different. "When William Hodge, a young New Light Presbyterian and one of the old boys of Caldwell's school, came with a warm presentation of the love and grace of God, saying little about the inescapable doom of the non-elect and preaching a gospel that anyone could accept without waiting for a miracle, Stone was promptly and soundly converted."[61]

Stone now "forgot his purpose to study law and decided that he would be a Presbyterian preacher, if he could be one like Hodge."[62] After completing his studies at Guilford Academy and while waiting for the next assembly of the Orange Presbytery to receive his license to preach, Stone visited his brother in Georgia. "His stay in that state was prolonged by an unexpected engagement to teach in Succoth Academy, a Methodist school at

---

56   Garrison/DeGroot, p. 93.
57   Ibid., p. 94.
58   Ibid., p. 94.
59   Ibid., p. 94.
60   West, p. 20.
61   Garrison/DeGroot, p. 94.
62   Ibid., p. 94.

Washington, Georgia, where he served as a 'professor of languages' for about one year, beginning in January of 1795".[63]

"The principal of the academy was Hope Hull, a Methodist minister who, before and during the conference of 1792, had supported O'Kelly's campaign against the Asbury autocracy. The principal and the young instructor (then aged 23) became firm friends".[64] What impressions Hull, who remained a Methodist, made on Stone are unknown, but it must be remembered that the O'Kelly Secession occurred in 1792, the Republican Methodist Church was formed in 1793, the Christian Church was established by O'Kelly in 1794, and the Hull/Stone friendship developed in 1795.

"Mention must also be made of John Springer, a New Light Presbyterian preacher of broad sympathies and ardently evangelistic temper, whose parish was only a few miles from Succoth Academy. Sectarian lines meant little to Springer. He had close fraternal relations with the neighboring Methodists and Baptists. He became one of Stone's most trusted friends and counselors. His influence on Stone, according to Stone's Carolina biographer, 'was decisive'".[65]

"The atmosphere in which Stone lived during that year was one in which denominational distinctions seemed unimportant, the niceties of traditional theology were forgotten, and the emphasis was upon the common core of the gospel".[66] Following this year in Georgia, Stone returned to North Carolina, where he received his license to preach. We must now study the working out Stone's thinking as it manifests itself in the revival atmosphere of Kentucky.

## Barton W. Stone: Preacher Who Rejects Calvinism

Stone returned from Georgia to North Carolina and on April 6, 1796, received his license to preach in the Presbyterian church, but was not yet ordained. By October of that year, he reached Kentucky and was installed as a regular supply minister of the two churches at Cane Ridge (seven miles east of Paris) and Concord (ten miles northeast of Cane Ridge). "The next year Stone was called to the settled pastorate of the two churches for which

---

63   Ibid., p. 94.
64   Ibid., p. 95.
65   Ibid., p. 95.
66   Ibid., p. 95.

he had been supplying. Acceptance of the call demanded ordination."[67] "The thought of his ordination led him to reexamine the Westminster Confession of Faith. He had some doubts and misgivings but was still in the process of thinking matters through."[68] Ordination demanded an acceptance of this creed.

"When the Transylvania Presbytery met in 1798 at Cane Ridge, Stone was asked: 'Do you receive and adopt the Confession of Faith, as containing the system of doctrine as taught in the Bible?' He replied, "I do, as far as I see it consistent with the word of God'". Oddly, he was accepted with this reservation and was ordained October 4, 1798. West notes, "one might well judge that Stone's respect for the Bible was increasing while his respect for human creeds was decreasing."[69]

"The Great Western Revival was a tidal wave of religious interest and excitement which began about 1800, reached its crest in 1803, and from that point gradually diminished in intensity and merged with the normal stream of evangelism, heightened by periodical camp meetings."[70] Such a camp meeting was planned in July of 1800 at the Gaspar River Church in Logan County, KY, where James McGready was now the pastor.

"Barton W. Stone decided to attend a camp meeting in Logan County in the spring of 1801. The extraordinary response of the people astounded him. He saw religion at a fever pitch; many people 'got religion' on the spot. Although Stone saw much in Logan County which he regarded as fanaticism, he became convinced that on balance the good far outweighed the bad."[71] Several of these camp meetings were held in southern and central Kentucky during 1801, but the "climax of the Bluegrass revival came at the Cane Ridge meeting ... it lasted from Friday to Wednesday, August 7–12, 1801."[72] "It has been estimated," West writes, "that from twenty to thirty thousand people were in attendance at the Great Revival at Cane Ridge. There were eighteen Presbyterian preachers plus some Methodists and Baptist preachers. Meetings were held on then Ridge at various spots and generally there were five or six preachers holding meetings at once."[73]

---

67  *Ibid.*, p. 98.
68  West, p. 22.
69  *Ibid.*, p. 22.
70  Garrison/DeGroot, p. 98.
71  McAllister/Tucker, p. 71.
72  Garrison/DeGroot, p. 101.
73  West, p. 23.

These meetings were characterized by strong physical reactions by those who "got religion"—"conversion was quite literally a convulsion".[74] People were known to scream, fall, and lay as dead; others developed jerks in various parts of their bodies; often jerks would progress to dancing that produced exhaustion and falling as dead; others would break forth with laughter and singing; some were said to bark like a dog as they fell to their knees and emitted grunting sounds.

"It wasn't long until the Presbytery began opposing the doctrines of the Cane Ridge Revival. The orthodox Presbyterians considered Stone a heretic. Their creed must be upheld at all costs. There were five men who came under the critical eye, men who substantially agreed in Stone's teaching. These were Barton W. Stone, Robert Marshall, Richard McNemar, John Dunlavy, and John Thompson."[75]

"About three months after the last amen had been spoken at the Cane Ridge Camp Meeting, three elders in the Cabin Creek Church in Kentucky accused their pastor, Richard McNemar, of advocating doctrines that contradicted the Bible and the Westminster Confession of Faith. He had 'expressly declared,' they reported, 'that a sinner has power to believe in Christ at any time,' and 'that Christ has purchased salvation for all the human race, without distinction.'"[76]

McNemar was condemned by the Washington Presbytery for "his 'Arminian views.' The case then came before the Synod of Kentucky, which had been formed in 1802 and which held its first meeting September 6–13, 1803. The Synod examined the report of the Washington Presbytery and sustained it."[77] "In the midst of the proceedings, Stone and his colleagues retired to formulate a proceeding of their own, knowing that McNemar's fate would soon be theirs. On Saturday, the tenth of September, they submitted their objection to the Synod because of the treatment of McNemar and declared themselves withdrawn from it" (*Ibid.*, p. 24).

Among the objections Stone, Marshall, Dunlavy, McNemar, and Thompson raised were: "We claim the privilege of interpreting the Scriptures by itself … and we believe that the Supreme Judge by whom all controversies of religion are to be determined … can be no other than the Holy Spirit speaking in the Scriptures."[78]

74　*Ibid.*, p. 24.
75　*Ibid.*, p. 24.
76　McAlister/Tucker, p. 73.
77　West, p. 24.
78　Garrison/DeGroot, p. 104.

"The five who had withdrawn from the Synod of Kentucky made it clear in their letter of withdrawal that they had not renounced Presbyterianism. In proof of this, they immediately organized the independent Springfield Presbytery".[79] The renunciation of Presbyterianism and the beginning of efforts to restore first-century Christianity were to begin the following year, 1804.

## Barton W. Stone: Christian Who Rejects Presbyterianism

Sometime in late 1803 or very early in 1804 Stone, Dunlavy, Marshall, McNemar, and Thompson published a defense of their views called *The Apology of the Springfield Presbytery*. It can be found in Stone's biography.[80] We will summarize it here:

First *The Apology* contains a Historical Introduction, Scriptural Defense, Consideration of Objections, Observations on the Confession of Faith, and Discussion of Creeds. What is noteworthy about *The Apology* is its appeal to the scriptures as the basis of truth.

*The Apology* defends:

- Free moral agency of sinners and their ability to know God.
- Regeneration by God through the word of truth.
- Christ died for all—not just the elect.
- Faith comes by the testimony and evidence of God's word—not by a miraculous working of grace.
- Faith can come "now" and need not wait for a special act of grace.
- Human creeds as a "standard" for teaching and practice cannot be justified.
- Rubbish of human tradition must be removed.

*The Apology* makes it clear that these men, though they still claim to be Presbyterians, cannot long remain in this "Calvinistic" fold.

The second major document of the Stone movement is called *The Last Will and Testament of the Springfield Presbytery*. It is a clear rejection of Presbyterianism and the beginning of a group that is variously called "Christians," the "Christian Church," or the "Church of Christ." Eight of the

---

79   Ibid., p. 105.
80   *The Biography of Elder Barton Warren Stone,* Barton W. Stone and John Rogers, p. 147–247.

twelve items are given in brief below.[81] The historic document was written June 28, 1804.

> IMPRIMIS (Firstly): "We will, what this body (Springfield Presbytery) die, be dissolved, and sink into union with the Body of Christ at large…"

> ITEM: "We will, that our name of distinction, with its Reverend title, be forgotten, that there be but one Lord over God's heritage, and his name One."

> ITEM: "We will, that our power of making laws for the government of the church, and executing them by delegated authority, forever cease; that the people may have free course to the Bible…"

> ITEM: "We will, that candidates for the Gospel ministry, henceforth study the Holy Scriptures with fervent prayer, and obtain license from God to preach the simple Gospel, with the Holy Ghost sent down from heaven, without any mixture of philosophy, vain deceit, traditions of men, or the rudiments of the world…"

> ITEM: "We will, that the church of Christ resume her native right of internal government…"

> ITEM: "We will, that in each particular church, as a body, actuated by the same spirit, choose her own preacher, admit members, and never delegate her right of government to any man or set of men whatever."

> ITEM: "We will, that people henceforth take the Bible as the only sure guide to heaven … for it is better to enter into life having one book, than having many to be cast into hell."

> ITEM: "We will, that our weak brethren, who may have been wishing to make the Presbytery of Springfield their king, …betake themselves to the Rock of Ages, and follow Jesus for the future."

What by mid-1804 Stone and his fellow preachers were advocating includes:

- The Bible as the sole authority and elimination of human creeds and the traditions of men.

---

81  Take from Historical Documents Advocating Christian Union, by C. A. Young, p. 21–22.

- Congregational independence and the removing of all governing bodies.
- Wearing the name Christian and the unity of all believers in one body.

"When the Springfield Presbytery had been dissolved, those who had been its members no longer considered themselves Presbyterians ... At that same meeting, June 28, 1804, it was agreed to adopt the name 'Christian,' to the exclusion of all sectarian names."[82]

Exactly ten years earlier, Rice Haggard had made a similar suggestion to O'Kelly and his associates when they were looking for a name to replace "Republican Methodist," and they adopted it. In his biography, Stone says, "We published a pamphlet on this name, written by Elder Rice Haggard, who had lately united with us."[83] "Quickly this new company of 'Christians' became a group of churches as well as an association of preachers." While it may be somewhat exaggerated—"It is reported that, with two exceptions, all the Presbyterian churches in southwestern Ohio became Christian."[84]

The final document that sets forth the views of Barton W. Stone is his monthly paper called *The Christian Messenger,* which was published in most years between 1826 and 1844. Its motto was "Let the Unity of Christians Be Our Polar Star." Stone was known to accept peculiar views regarding the 'trinity,' the nature of Christ, and the atonement. He was, however, of an irenic spirit and unwilling to insist upon these ideas to the point of division.

"At first, Stone gave little attention to the subject of baptism. He even considered it an optional practice. When controversy arose among his followers, he finally began a study of the Scriptures which led him to the conclusion that immersion of believers was the divinely ordained baptism, and he himself was immersed. Thereafter he began to preach that baptism 'is ordained by the King,' and that the Bible clearly taught the ordinance was 'for the remission of sins.' Most Christians in Kentucky became strictly immersionists. He opposed the practice of excluding the un-immersed from Communion and fellowship, however, and urged 'patience and forbearance toward such pious persons as cannot be convinced' they should be immersed."[85]

Stone did not meet Alexander Campbell until 1824. We shall consider their relationship and the relationship of the two groups after our study of the Campbells.

---

82  Garrison/DeGroot, p. 111.
83  Stone/Rogers, p. 50.
84  Garrison/DeGroot, p. 112.
85  *Christians Only,* James DeForest Murch, p. 93.

# Conclusion

Barton W. Stone died November 9, 1844, and received the following eulogy from the pen of Tobert Fanning:

> The history of Brother Stone would be the history of the most important religious movements in the United States, for nearly a half century ... To be sure his talent was not, perhaps, quite so brilliant as some others; but his acquaintance with the scriptures was extensive and critical, and a more humble, conscientious, and pious man cannot be found. If justice is ever done to his memory, he will be regarded as the first great American reformer, the first man, who, to much purpose, pleaded the ground that the Bible without not, commentary or creed, must destroy antichristian powers, and eventually conquer the world."[86]

Although Stone was often slandered and his views sometimes perverted, Fanning says:

> Yet never did I hear mortal man utter a syllable derogatory to his moral worth. A man more devoted to Christianity has not lived nor died, and many stars will adorn his crown in a coming day.[87]

"It is frequently asked, 'Why so much zeal in the present day against authoritative creeds, party names, and party spirits?' I answer for myself: 'because I am assured, they stand in the way of Christian union, and are contrary to the will of God.' It is again asked, 'Why so zealous for Christian union?' I answer, 'because I firmly believe that Jesus fervently prayed to his Father as sent by the Father ... if we oppose the union of believers, we directly oppose the will of God, the prayer of Jesus, the spirit of piety, and the salvation of the world. If we contend for party creeds, party names, and party spirits, we contend for disunion, for these are among the chief causes of it.'"[88]

---

86   West, p. 34–35.
87   *Ibid.*, p. 34–35.
88   *Christian Messenger*, Barton W. Stone, Vol. 1, 1826, p. 15–16.

# Discussion

1. What religious group did Stone first join? What did he eventually have problems with? By 1832, how many had obeyed the gospel in the so-called Stone movement?

2. When was Stone born? Where? Where was he educated? What did he study? What were his ultimate plans originally? What came to the academy that greatly influenced his life? What principal revivalists did he hear? Who licensed Stone to preach? How may he have related to O'Kelly?

3. Where did Stone go to from North Carolina? Where did he preach in Kentucky? What unusual happened at his ordination? Where did Stone learn of the Great Western Revival? What important event occurred at the Cane Ridge Church? What were some of the physical effects at the revival at Cane Ridge? Who had problems with the Presbyterians? Why? Who joined McNemar in his withdrawal from the Presbytery? What did these men form?

4. In what did men of the Springfield Presbytery defend their views? What were some of those views? What did they write the following year? Summarize the views of the *Last Will*. What did these men now call themselves? Who connects Stone with O'Kelly's ideas? What was Stone's paper called? What subjects in it were sources of controversy? How did he view baptism?

5. When did Stone die? How would you assess his ability and character? What were his principal emphases?

# Chapter 6

# Declaration and Address: Thomas Campbell

## Introduction

Thomas Campbell, who came to America from Ireland in 1807, is viewed by many as the "patriarch" or "father" of the Restoration movement. The *Declaration and Address*, written by Thomas Campbell in 1809, is the earliest definitive statement of the principles of "unity" through "restoration"—the twin themes of the Restoration movement. Although Thomas Campbell took a back seat to his son Alexander, he propounded the essential theme of the movement that his son and many others only expounded. Campbell's famous Biblical motto, *where the scriptures speak, we speak; where the scriptures are silent, we are silent,* became the foundation upon which all others built.

In this lesson we will look at Thomas Campbell's life, the beginning of the Christian Association of Washington, and his Declaration and Address.

## Thomas Campbell: Religious Background and Early Influences

Thomas Campbell was of Scottish lineage but was born and reared in Ireland. He was born in County Down, Ireland, February 1, 1763. His ancestors were Scotch, and several generations before had moved from Scotland to the north of Ireland.[89] Campbell was the son of a Roman Catholic who had turned Anglican. His own deeply devout nature found more congenial association among the Presbyterians, who were numerous in north Ireland because of migrations from Scotland.[90]

In preparation for the ministry Campbell "took the full three-year classical course at the University of Glasgow and followed this with the training provided by the theological seminary of the Anti-burgher division of the Seceder branch of the Presbyterian church."[91] The divisive, splintered background of the Presbyterians is important in understanding Campbell's interest on "restoration" and "unity."

---

89   Historical Documents Advocating Christian Union, C. A. Young, p. 27.
90   Garrison/DeGroot, p. 124.
91   *Ibid.*, p. 124.

The Seceder branch of the Presbyterian church had withdrawn from the Church of Scotland in 1733 in protest over certain aspects of the connection between church and government, especially against the "patronage" system, under which the right of appointing ministers belonged, not to parish, session, or presbytery, but to lay landlords. The Seceders soon divided into two parties, Burghers and Anti-Burghers, on the issue as to whether or not the members of their communion could properly subscribe to the oath imposed by law upon any who would become burgesses (delegates in a borough). During the time of Thomas Campbell's ministry in Ireland each of the two parties was again divided into "Old-Lights" and "New-Lights" on another obscure and minute point involved in church-state relations. Mr. Campbell was an Old-Light Anti-Burgher Seceder Presbyterian.[92] As Homer Hailey notes, "Such bigotry and narrowness had the effect of moving him to seek unity wherever he labored."[93] Thomas Campbell's experience with this specific manifestation of the sectarian spirit…turned his mind permanently toward Christian union.[94]

Campbell preached and taught several places, but in 1798 became the settled minister of Ahorey church, with which he remained until he left for America in 1807. The Ahorey church was in the open country, about two miles from the rather substantial town of Rich Hill, thirty miles southwest of Belfast.[95] At Rich Hill, Campbell taught in an academy where he educated many young men, including his son Alexander. Already familiar with the writings of Glas, Sandeman, and J. A. Haldane, Campbell met the church at Rich Hill, a "church of the type often called "Scotch Independent," embodying the principles of Glas, Sandeman, and strongly influenced by the ideas of the Haldanes … here he met and heard the celebrated English evangelist Rowland Hill … whose evangelizing tours were partly financed by the Haldane brothers. To Rich Hill also came the eccentric John Walker of Dublin, who made so much of precisely following the precepts and precedents of Scripture that he resigned a fellowship in Trinity College and left the Anglican church to lead an independent movement."[96]

Campbell read and conducted his son Alexander in a study of John Locke's essays concerning "Toleration" and "Human Understanding." He found in the *Letters Concerning Toleration* "an appeal for nonsectarian Christianity,

---

92  Ibid., p. 127.
93  Attitudes and Consequences of the Restoration Movement, Homer Hailey, p. 47.
94  Garrison/DeGroot, p. 127.
95  Ibid., p. 125.
96  Ibid., p. 128.

though from a different approach."⁹⁷ Locke "began by urging that the state, even though it had an established church, should grant full toleration to dissenting religious groups ... So, he ended by demanding that the church should tolerate varieties of opinion and practice within itself, finding its bond of unity in the few essential things which Christ and his apostles had made essential."⁹⁸

After spending several years teaching at Rich Hill, in addition to his labors as "pastor" of a congregation there (Ahorey), Mr. Campbell's health began to fail. Finally, after having been warned by his physician that he must make some change in his program of work, he was persuaded by his friends and son, Alexander, to seek health in America.⁹⁹ Campbell left Ireland on the first of April 1807.

# Thomas Campbell: American and the Christian Association

On May 13, 1807, Thomas Campbell stepped from the boat at Philadelphia into the meeting of the Associate Synod of North America, then in session in that city. (This synod represented all the Seceder Presbyterian churches in America.) After only two days, he was appointed to the Presbytery of Chartiers, in southwest Pennsylvania. "Campbell found his brethren in America characterized by the same narrowness of the Old World. He disregarded their intolerant practices in his pastoral ministrations and drew upon him the censure of his Presbytery for the exercise of too great Christian liberty and charity toward other religious bodies."¹⁰⁰ The incident that provoked the censure was the serving of communion to others than "Seceder Presbyterians."

This prompted a long and complicated trial that stretched through 1808 into 1809. Following the censure, Campbell was eventually suspended and then expelled from the Presbyterian church, officially on May 23, 1809. They, however, continued to deal with him until April 17, 1810, when "accordingly the Presbytery did and hereby do depose Mr. Campbell from the office of the Holy Ministry and from sealing ordinances."¹⁰¹ For about a year after his withdrawal from the Presbytery and synod, (September 13, 1808) Thomas Campbell continued to preach, as opportunity offered, in private

---

97   Ibid., p. 128.
98   Ibid, p. 129.
99   Hailey, p. 48.
100  Young, p. 30–31.
101  Garrison/Degroot, p. 139. See p. 129–139.

houses in the area where he had itinerated, and especially in the vicinity of Washington, Pennsylvania.[102] During that time he organized no independent church and made no effort to draw either ministers or laymen away from the Presbyterian church.[103]

A group of earnest Christians gathered to discuss future plans in the home of Abraham Altars early in the summer of 1809. Thomas Campbell led the meeting in prayer and proceeded to review their reasons for the gathering. He dwelt at length on the views resulting from divisions within the scriptures. Everything in religion not found in the Bible was to be abandoned so that a basis for Christian union could be formed. Bringing his message to a close, he put into simple terms the principle he understood the group to be acting on. "That rule, my highly respected hearers," he said, "is this, that where the scriptures speak, we speak; where the scriptures are silent, we are silent."[104] From this meeting Campbell conceived the idea of forming a Christian Association, which would not be a church but an agency for helping propagate the ideas of Christian cooperation. At a second meeting held August 17, 1809, it was decided to organize "The Christian Association of Washington," after the county in which the association proposed to be active.[105]

As noted above, the Association was not a church. It had no intention of becoming a church. So, the Christian Association would be an independent society working for reform in and through the churches, probably having members who were members of various churches, and certainly not forming another church. To express more fully the principles and objectives of the Christian Association, Thomas Campbell prepared a brief "declaration" and a more extended "address." These were presented to the Association at a subsequent meeting as the report of a committee of twenty-one … on September 7, 1809, the Association voted approval of this document and ordered that it be printed.[106]

# Thomas Campbell: Principles of the Declaration and Address

The theme of Campbell's essay is summarized in his own expression, *Scriptural Unity*. It calls for the unity of all Christians and churches based on

---

102 West, p. 46.
103 Garrison/DeGroot, p. 139.
104 *Ibid.*, p. 139.
105 McAllister/Tucker, p. 110.
106 Garrison/DeGroot, p. 140.

the scriptures alone. The treatise, depending on the print size, contains from around 80–140 pages and is divided into a *declaration,* and *address,* and an *appendix.* Young's account (which we are using) contains 139 pages.

## Declaration

A brief introduction of eight pages declaring the formation of the Christian Association of Washington (Pennsylvania), the goals of the Association, and nine resolutions related to organizing and sustaining the Association.

1. To form a religious association "for the sole purpose of promoting simple evangelical Christianity, free from all mixture of human opinions and inventions of men."
2. A call for members to financially support a pure gospel ministry, that shall reduce to practice that whole form of doctrine, worship, discipline, and government, expressly revealed, and enjoined in the word of God.
3. To encourage the formation of similar associations for similar purposes.
4. That this society by no means considers itself a church … but merely as voluntary advocates for church reformation.
5. That this society, formed for the sole purpose of promoting simple evangelical Christianity, shall … support such ministers… such as to reduce to practice that simple original form of Christianity, expressly exhibited on the sacred page; without attempting to inculcate anything of human authority, or private opinion, or inventions of men,… or anything as a matter of Christian faith and duty, for which there cannot be expressly produced a *thus saith the Lord,* either in express terms, or by approved precedent.
6. That a standing committee of twenty-one members … be chosen annually to superintend the interests and transact the business of the Society.
7. That this Society meet at least twice a year, viz.: on the first Thursday of May, and of November.
8. That each meeting of the Society be opened with a sermon, the constitution and address read, and a collection lifted for the benefit of the Society; and that all communications of a public nature be laid before the Society at its half-yearly meetings.
9. That the Society, relying upon the all-sufficiency of the Church's Head … holds itself engage to afford a competent support to such ministers as the Lord may graciously dispose to assist, at the request, and by invitation of the Society, in promoting a pure evangelical reformation, by the simple preaching of the everlasting gospel, and the administration

of its ordinances in an exact conformity to the Divine standard as aforesaid.[107]

What is clearly promoted in these resolutions are the twin themes of the movement—unity and restoration. This, the resolutions emphasize, can be accomplished by the scriptures alone, accepting the express teaching of the Bible and eliminating human opinions.

## *Address*

"A repetitive plea, yea, a cry, calling on that love our Lord Jesus Christ, in sincerity, throughout all the churches, to join in the work for an entire union of all the churches in faith and practice, according to the word of God."[108]

Restating with greater clarity and emphasis the principles of the *declaration*, the *address* sets forth thirteen propositions in 49 pages.

1. That the Church of Christ upon earth is essentially, intentionally, and constitutionally one; consisting of all those in every place that profess their faith in Christ and obedience to him in all things according to the scriptures.
2. That the Church consists of many particular local groups, yet there should be no schisms among them. They ought all walk by the same rule and speak the same things.
3. That to do this, nothing ought to be inculcated upon Christians as articles of faith; nor required of them as terms of communion, but what is expressly taught and enjoined upon them in the word of God.
4. That although the scriptures of the Old and New Testaments are inseparably connected, the New Testament is as perfect a constitution for the worship, discipline, and government of the New Testament church as the Old Testament was for the Old Testament church.
5. Where the scriptures are silent…no human authority has power to interfere, to supply the supposed deficiency by making laws for the church.
6. Inferences and deductions can edify the church, but no such deductions can be made terms of communion … it is evident that such deductions or inferential truths ought to have any place in the church's confession.
7. Doctrinal exhibitions and defenses must be in a great measure the effect of human reasoning, and of course must contain many inferential truths, hence, they ought not be made terms of Christian communion.

---

107 Young, p. 74–78.
108 *Ibid.*, p. 91.

8. Acceptance into the church must not be based upon understanding of all Divine truth, but upon knowledge of one's lost and perishing condition … and of the way salvation through Jesus Christ, accompanied with a profession of their faith and obedience to him, in all things, according to his word.
9. All who make this profession should love each other as brethren, children of the same family and father, temples of the same spirit, members of the same body.
10. That division among the Christians is a horrid evil, fraught with many evils. It is antichristian, as it destroys the visible unity of the body of Christ. It is likewise anti-scriptural and anti-natural.
11. That (in some instances) a partial neglect of the expressly revealed word of God, and (in others) an assumed authority for making the approbation of human opinions and human inventions a term of communion … are, and have been, the immediate, obvious, and universally acknowledged causes, of all the corruptions and divisions that ever have taken place in the church of God.
12. None are to be received or retained in the church who do not profess their faith in Christ and obey him in all things, according to the scriptures. Also, that ministers must inculcate none other things than those very articles of faith and holiness expressly revealed and enjoined in the word of God. Lastly, that in all their administrations they keep close by the observance of all Divine ordinances, after the example of the primitive church, exhibited in the New Testament, without any additions whatsoever of human opinions or inventions of men.
13. Human expedients can be employed only if they are absolutely necessary, but must not be viewed as of sacred origin, so that any subsequent alteration or difference in the observance of these things might produce no contention nor division in the church.[109]

Once again, the essential elements of Campbell's views are Unity of all churches; restoration of the primitive church; acceptance of the Bible alone as a standard of faith and practice; elimination of human opinions and inventions of men. Young mentions that to prepare the way for a permanent scripture unity among Christians, by calling up to their consideration fundamental truths, directing their attention to first principles, clearing the way before them by removing the stumbling blocks, the rubbish of the ages, which has been thrown upon it, and fencing it on each side, that in advancing toward the desired object they may not miss the way through mistake or

---

[109] Ibid., p. 107–114.

inadvertency, by turning aside to the right hand or to the left, is, at least, the sincere intention of the above prepositions.[110]

## *Appendix*

This is a laborious effort over 81 pages to explain himself and his views more fully and to answer objections that might be raised against the *declaration and address*. It adds nothing of real substance to the above resolutions and propositions.

# Conclusion

In the *Declaration* and *Address*, Campbell does not deal with specific issues, but lays down the principles for "restoration" and "unity." He himself had not envisioned fully where these principles would lead and what beliefs and practices must now be eliminated. It would be left to his son Alexander to define more specifically what this message demands.

An example of how this message would affect their present views occurred immediately following the delivery of the *Declaration* and *Address*, when Thomas Campbell sat down. A Scottish bookseller, Andrew Munro, a rather sentimental person was the first to break the silence. "Mr. Campbell," he said, "if we adopt *that* as a basis, then there is an end of infant baptism." Campbell replied, "Of course, if infant baptism be not found in the scriptures, we can have nothing to do with it." Thomas Acheson then arose and cried: "I hope I may never see the day when my heart will renounce that blessed saying of the Scripture, "Suffer little children to come unto me and forbid them not, for of such is the kingdom of heaven." Saying that, he burst into tears. James Foster, who even in Ireland had been opposed to infant baptism, arose, and cried out, "Mr. Acheson, I would remark that in the portion of Scripture you have quoted, *there is no reference whatever to infant baptism.*"[111]

Thomas Campbell was an irenic, lovable gentleman in character and was not the personality necessary to press these issues and carry through with this reform, as it was then called. His *Declaration* and *Address* reveals how tortured he was by the sectarian division and party strife of his days, but his kindly spirit was not what this work demanded. It was left to his son Alexander, whom we will look at next, to confront the division and challenge the religious word to, as he put it, "restore the ancient order of things."

---

110 *Ibid.*, p. 115.
111 West, p. 48. See also *Memoirs of Alexander Campbell*, Robert Richardson, Vol. 1, p. 238.

# Discussion

1. How is Thomas Campbell's relation to the Restoration Movement sometimes described? When did he come to America? What document did he write that is so important? What famous motto or slogan did he give the movement?

2. What was Thomas' ancestry? Where was he born and reared? When was he born? What was he religiously? Describe his education. What kind of Presbyterian was he? How did the party strife affect him? Where did he preach? Where did he have a school? What men did he meet who influenced him? What philosopher influenced him?

3. When did Thomas arrive in America? Where was he assigned as a minister? What did he find religion like in America? After a long trial what happened to him? When did this occur? What did he find it necessary to form? What was the motto of the Association? What celebrated document did he write?

4. What three sections did this document contain? What are the twin themes of the Restoration Movement that this document highlights? List four principles that summarize the teaching of this document.

5. What issue exemplifies the kinds of issues this document did not anticipate? Describe the disposition of Thomas Campbell. Who would give definition to the principles stated by Thomas Campbell?

**Chapter 7**

# A Restoration of the Ancient Order: Alexander Campbell

## Introduction

If Thomas Campbell's *Declaration* and *Address* enunciated the principles of "restoration" and "unity" in the religious world, his son Alexander's *Christian Baptist,* a monthly periodical, defined specifically the nature of the two concepts. If Thomas Campbell was disposed to be irenic and peaceful, his son Alexander was inclined to be both confrontational and controversial.

It was Alexander Campbell, as a superb preacher, analytical debater, and prolific writer, who stepped forth to challenge Catholicism, skepticism, and sectarianism. He, more than any other, gave impetus and national significance to what he called "a restoration of the order of things."

In this chapter we will look at the life of Alexander Campbell up to 1830, observing his "preparation to preach," "the beginning of controversy," and "avenues of propagation."

## Alexander Campbell: Preparation to Preach

Alexander Campbell was born in Antrim County Ireland. His father, Thomas Campbell, having married Jane Corneigle in June 1787, was blessed with his first child, Alexander, born on September 12, 1788. As a minister in the Seceder Presbyterian church, Thomas Campbell was instructed by the Synod to "worship God in his family" by singing, reading, and prayer, morning, and evening; that he should catechize and instruct them at least once a week in religion—all of which he was "carefully observant." In their family was also a rule that "every member should memorize, during each day, some portion of the Bible, to be recited at evening worship."[112]

On the Lord's Day—Every member of the house was expected to go to meeting, and it was understood that each one was to give, upon returning home, an account not only of the text, but of the discourse itself, embracing

---
112  Richardson, p. 35.

its leading points. It was under such influences in the domestic circle that Alexander Campbell passed his early years; and it cannot be doubted that they had a most important bearing on his future life.[113]

Alexander Campbell studied at a couple of elementary schools, but his principal education came at the insistence and guidance of his father who opened an academy in Rich Hill to compliment his salary as a minister. Well educated and a teacher of high repute, Thomas Campbell directed Alexander in the studies of Greek, Latin, French, English Literature, Philosophy, etc. Alexander had become so proficient in the various branches of learning that by age 17, his father used him as an assistant in his Rich Hill Academy. By this time books were his constant delight, and self-education became with him a passion, as there seems but little prospect of his being enabled to attend the University, owing to his father's large family. His father had enough confidence in the ability of his son that he left him in charge of the academy when he embarked for America in April 1807. Alexander was then 19 years old.[114]

Thomas Campbell, now in America, had written urging his family to join him. They traveled to Londonderry in September 1808 and tried three times to embark. In October at Londonderry they had taken passage on an ill-fated ship which was wrecked off the coast of Scotland. For various reasons, but especially because it would permit Alexander to take courses at the university, the family decided to winter in Glasgow. They stayed in Glasgow until August 1809 when they had taken ship for New York.[115]

The providential experience of the shipwreck, Campbell always believed it was exactly that, enabled him to enter Glasgow University for his long-cherished encounter with higher education. Almost immediately, Alexander contacted Greville Ewing, minister of the Independent church, whose acquaintance he had formed on a visit to Rich Hill.[116] Mr. Ewing formed a strong attachment to the young university student and invited him to his home for discussions and for special gatherings. Greville Ewing, you may recall, was the one who rand the seminary of the Haldanes at Glasgow and who emphasized scriptural authority, congregational independence, weekly observance of the Lord's Supper, etc.[117]

---

113  Ibid., p. 36.
114  Ibid., p. 47, 76, 87.
115  McAlister/Tucker, p. 115.
116  *Christians Only,* James Deforest Murch, p. 55–56.
117  Garrison/DeGroot, p. 51.

By the influences on Campbell at Glasgow, he seceded from the Seceder Presbyterian Church before he came to America and learned of his father's exclusion from that body. From Greville Ewing, Campbell's close friend, the latter borrowed an intensely independent spirit. At once, he began to examine for himself, the claims of the Seceder Church as a religious group. Slowly, he was led to doubt them. The crucial hour came at the semi-annual communion service, near the close of his stay in Glasgow. It was the custom to give all who were to partake of the Lord's Supper a metallic token to shut out the unworthies from partaking. As Campbell had come from Ireland without any letter of recommendation, it was necessary for him to take an examination before the elders on a Saturday to determine his worthiness. He took the examination and passed. But on the next day, his conscience hurt him. He put his token in the plate that morning and refused to partake of the communion. Campbell had now crossed the Rubicon; he was no longer with the Seceder Church.[118]

On July 31, 1809, Campbell left Glasgow for Greenock. Four days later, he and his family were on the ship *Latonia*, headed for America. This time the trip went smoothly. The ship landed at New York on Friday, September 29. The following Thursday, they left New York for Philadelphia in the direction of Washington. Thomas Campbell, who had learned of their coming, had left his home in Washington, going toward Philadelphia. On the way, the two parties met. Thomas Campbell fondly embraced his family, and they in return had their spirits renewed within them by this reunion.[119]

Having both left the Seceder Presbyterian church and finding themselves of one accord they soon discussed the *Declaration* and *Address,* which had already been proclaimed, ordered to be printed, and was not being readied for publication. Alexander read his father's writing with great interest and gave his hearty approval. He shared with his father how he was determined to devote his life to proclaiming the principles contained therein. At his father's insistence, Alexander then devoted the next six months to disciplined study of the Scriptures. His first sermon, delivered July 15, 1810, was enthusiastically received by a large congregation. Alexander himself realized that he had found his true vocation. From that day forward, his services were in continual demand; that first year he preached no less than 106 sermons.[120]

---

118  West, p. 52.
119  West, p. 52.
120  See McAllister/Tucker, p. 115–16 and West, p. 53.

# Alexander Campbell: Beginning of Controversy

Though Thomas Campbell has been dismissed as a minister in the Seceder Presbyterian church and had now formed the Christian Association of Washington, he decided to apply to the Synod of Pittsburgh for membership of the association in the regular Presbyterian church. He and his followers were rejected in the fall session, October 2, 1810.

After the Synod's rejection, Thomas Campbell, still opposed to controversy, was willing to let matters rest as they were. Alexander, however, soon convinced members of the Christian Association that some answer would have to be made to the Synod. He decided to make the next meeting of the Association, scheduled for November, the occasion for a public reply.[121]

As his texts he used Isaiah 57.14 and 62.10, a passage he would apply to casting up and removing the stumbling block of human opinions. His sermon is summarized thusly:

1. The chief objective of the new reformation is to persuade Christians to abandon human statements and adopt "the form of sound words" as the true "basis of union."
2. Each congregation should have its own internal government by elders and deacons and, while regarded as an independent body, should have fellowship with other churches of like faith.
3. The distinction between clergy and laity is unauthorized by scripture and should be abandoned.
4. Infant baptism is without direct scriptural authority, but the practice should be a matter of forbearance.
5. Should religious parties refuse to accept the overtures of the Christian Association, it might be necessary to resolve it into a distinct church or congregation in order for members to carry out for themselves the duties and obligations laid upon them by the Holy Spirit.
6. The principle of receiving or practicing nothing but what was expressly taught in the scriptures was likely to result in the abandonment of many things deemed precious and important by existing churches.[122]

## *The Brush Run Church*

The Christian Association, meeting on May 4, 1811, constituted itself as a church with a congregational form of government. At this same meeting, Thomas was chosen as an elder and Alexander was licensed to preach;

---

121 McAllister/Tucker, p. 116.
122 Murch, p. 58; McAllister/Tucker, p. 117.

ordination to Christian ministry came January 1, 1812. A building was needed for worship and the site selected was on the farm of William Gilcrist, in the valley of Brush Run, about two miles above the junction of that stream with Buffaloe Creek.[123] It was subsequently known as the "Brush Run Church." The building itself was an 18' by 36' frame and the first service was held on June 16, 1811, with the interior still unfinished.[124]

## *Baptism*

After the formation of the Brush Run Church, it was noticed that two or three of the members did not partake of the Lord's Supper with the rest. On being questioned they replied that they did not consider themselves to be authorized to partake since they had never been baptized. This raised the question of baptism in a most practical way. Thomas Campbell still objected to "rebaptism," but these had not even been sprinkled in infancy and they wanted him to immerse them. This he did, on July 4, 1811, in Buffaloe Creek. After his incident it seems to have been agreed that immersion only would be practiced for adults who had not been previously sprinkled, but the question as to whether infants should be sprinkled was still open.[125]

On March 13, 1812, Alexander's first child, Jane, was born, and with her birth he began to restudy the whole question of baptism… painstakingly he sought out the meaning of "baptize" in Greek and became convinced it means "to immerse." He became certain that the sprinkling to which he had been subjected to in infancy was unauthorized by the scriptures, and that he was consequently an unbaptized person. Furthermore, he could not consistently preach immersion and remain unimmersed. Alexander, Thomas and his wife, and Alexander's sister were all baptized in Buffaloe Creek June 12, 1812.[126]

## *Redstone Association*

The adoption of immersion by the "reformers" as they were soon called, erected a barrier between them and other churches, especially the Presbyterians. One result of the adoption of immersion was to bring Brush Run Church into more friendly relations with the Baptists. In their preaching and visiting across the countryside, Thomas and Alexander Campbell became acquainted with the various Baptist congregations and their

---

123  McAllister/Tucker, p. 117.
124  Garrison/DeGroot, p. 156.
125  Garrison/DeGroot, p. 159–60; Richardson, p. 371–72; McAllister/Tucker, p. 118.
126  McAllister/Tucker, p.118.

ministers, who often urged them to join their association. The Campbells, however, had several objections to such a union. Brush Run did not accept the strongly Calvinistic Philadelphia Confession of Faith. It differed on the place of the New Testament in relation to the Bible. It also differed on the qualifications necessary for baptism as well as its purpose. Finally, there were disagreements over the frequency of communion.[127]

After profound discussion over the fall of 1813, the Brush Run Church applied for admission to the Redstone Baptist Association. In doing so it submitted a full statement of its sentiments, in eight or ten pages. This document has not been preserved unfortunately, but it is known that it included an reiteration of the protest against creeds, and expressed a willingness to join the association only "provided always that we should be allowed to teach and preach whatever we learned from the Holy Scriptures, regardless of any human creed."[128]

## *Sermon on Law*

In the Redstone Association from the start there was minority opposition to the Campbells and the Brush Run Church. And Alexander's celebrated "Sermon on Law" only added to the provocation and irritation. A novel idea in 1816 when Campbell delivered it to the Redstone Association meeting at Cross Creek on August 30, it was his declaration of independence for the whole Christian church as against the entire system of Old Testament law. He sought to show that the Christian gospel is a new institution and not an extension and modification of the Hebrew legal system. He affirmed that with the coming of Christ, the law was done away, not merely ceremonial law, but the whole law. Finally, he asserted that all such Old Testament practices as baptizing infants (in place of circumcision), paying tithes, observing holy days and fasts, such as the one in preparation for the Lord's Supper, sanctifying the seventh day, and establishing any form of religion by civil law are "repugnant to Christianity."[129]

Alexander Campbell, young and zealous, was now the leader of this movement of reform, and was soon to make it a movement of restoration. Seeds of controversy were being sown as he sought avenues to propagate these Biblical views.

---

127 McAlister/Tucker, p. 120.
128 Garrison/DeGroot, p. 161.
129 *Ibid.*, p. 165–66.

# Alexander Campbell: Avenues of Propagation

## Buffalo Seminary 1818–23

As assistant and instructor at the Rich Hill Academy and student at the University of Glasgow, Alexander was well qualified to establish a seminary, which he did for boys on his own farm in 1818. His purpose was especially to find and train material for the ministry. He took the students into his own home, boarded them at his own table, and taught them personally.[130] The seminary failed to attract a significant number of students for the ministry and was closed in 1823. After five years as school master Alexander had decided on other approaches to the dissemination of his views.

## Debates

Intelligent, educated, analytical, Alexander after much persuasion agreed to his first debate in 1820 at Mt. Pleasant, PA with John Walker, a Seceder Presbyterian. The subject was baptism. Mr. Walker affirmed the preposition that the infant children of believers are proper subjects, and that sprinkling is a proper mode or action.[131] Campbell was so successful in this medium of teaching that, though sparingly, it became for him an accepted avenue of teaching restoration ideas.

### Maccalla Debate

Campbell next accepted a challenge for debate from E. L. Maccalla of August, KY. He was also a Seceder Presbyterian and affirmed infant baptism and sprinkling are divine institutions. The debate with Maccalla covered much of the same ground as the Walker debate with one major difference—Campbell came out more plainly on the design of baptism.

One of Campbell's arguments against infant sprinkling was drawn from the design of baptism; for since its purpose is the remission of sins, it was never intended for the infant. This emphasis on the scriptural design of baptism was undoubtedly the most significant contribution of the Campbell-Maccalla debate, and it sounded as heretical to Baptist ears as Campbell's distinction between the covenants had sounded during the Walker debate. Campbell had stated in the Walker debate that baptism related to the promise of the remission of sins, and the gift of the Holy Spirit, but he made

---

130  *Ibid.*, p. 168.
131  *Ibid.*, p. 168–69.

no effort to expand this belief statement into an argument, and apparently did not grasp its monumental import.[132]

Said Campbell in the debate, "Its great significance may be seen from the following testimonies: 'He that believeth and is BAPTIZED shall be saved.' He does not say, he that believeth, and keeps my commandments, shall be saved; but he saith 'He that believeth and is baptized shall be saved.' He placeth baptism on the right hand of faith. Again, he tells Nicodemus, that 'except a man be born of water and of the Spirit, he cannot enter into the kingdom of God,' Peter, on the day of Pentecost, places baptism in the same exalted place: 'Repent,' says he, 'and be baptized every one of you, FOR the remission of sins.' Ananias saith to Paul, 'Arise, and be baptized, and WASH AWAY your sins, calling upon the name of the Lord.'"[133]

## Owen Debate

The debate in 1829 with the internationally known infidel Robert Owen did much to bring Alexander to national prominence. The debate was conducted in Cincinnati, Ohio, August 13–21. It really was not much of a debate. Owen arose each speech to read what he called the twelve laws of human nature which he argued prove that "men are not morally responsible for their actions and are not subjects of praise or criticism or reward or punishment. Guided by the remorseless force of circumstances, an individual cannot think, act, love, hate or do anything other than that he does."[134] These laws he affirmed disprove all religion. Campbell offered objections to the twelve laws which Owen ignored, so Campbell spent his time developing evidences for the truthfulness of Christianity. To these Owen responded by rereading his twelve laws.

## Purcell Debate

The Sycamore Street Church in Cincinnati hosted a debate between Campbell and Catholic Bishop John Baptist Purcell January 13–21, 1837. It was viewed as a "Protestant vs. Catholic" debate, but Campbell made clear that only upon the basis of New Testament Christianity, that represented by the Restoration Movement, could one defeat the claims of Roman hierarchy; and he stated emphatically throughout the discussion that he defended the Bible and was bound by no other creed of Christendom.[135] Since Campbell

---

132  Campbell and Controversy, The Debates of Alexander Campbell, Bill J. Humble, p. 180.
133  *Ibid.*, p. 181.
134  Humble, p. 97.
135  *Ibid.*, p. 131.

and Purcell covered the major errors of Catholicism, the debate furnished Campbell a public platform and both a Protestant and Catholic audience for the furtherance of restoration aims.

## Rice Debate

Nathan Lewis Rice, a Presbyterian, had gained a reputation as a religious debate and became the opponent of Alexander Campbell in his last debate, beginning November 15, 1843, and continuing through the next 16 days. The discussion was held in the Main Street Church building at Lexington, KY. It, though of higher quality, was a continuation of the Walker/Maccalla Debates on the nature, mode, and design of baptism. It also took up the questions of creeds, the operation of the Spirit through the word, and whether only a bishop can administer baptism. Rice, according to Humble, "proved to be the most difficult opponent whom Campbell ever encountered in public discussion.[136] And yet the debate proved in print, where debate tactics prove useless, to be a disappointment and of little value to the Presbyterian cause.

## *The Christian Baptist*

The *Christian Baptist*, a monthly periodical edited and published by Alexander Campbell, was a principal means of propagating restoration ideas from August 3, 1823, to July 5, 1830. It, more than any other avenue, defined specifically what restoration entailed. It was a small magazine, but it was immensely important in disseminating Mr. Campbell's views, furnishing a rallying point for those who accepted his ideas of reformation, precipitating the separation from the Baptists, and setting the pattern of thought among his followers for many years thereafter.[137] "A Restoration of the Ancient Order of Things" is the title of a series of 32 articles that began February 7, 1825 and continued intermittently throughout the remaining years of the publication. In this opening article Campbell decries "reformation" and speaks of a need for "restoration." Writes Campbell:

> All reformations in religious opinion and speculations have been fated like the fashions in apparel. They have lived, and died, and revived, and died again… Every attempt to reform Christianity is like an attempt to create a new sun, or to change the revolutions of the heavenly bodies—unprofitable and vain. In a word we have had reformations enough. The very name has become as offensive, as the term 'Revolution' in France. A restoration of the

---

136  *Ibid.*, p. 194.
137  Garrison/DeGroot, p. 175.

ancient order of things is all that is necessary to the happiness and usefulness of Christians ... to bring the societies of Christians up to the New Testament, is just to bring the disciples individually and collectively, to walk in the faith, and the commandments of the Lord and Savior, as presented in that blessed volume; and this is to restore the ancient order of things. Celebrated as the era of restoration is, we doubt not but that the era of restoration will as far transcend it in importance and fame, though the long and blissful Millennium, as the New Testament transcends in simplicity, beauty, excellency, and majesty, the dogmas and notions of the creed of Westminster and the canons of the Assembly's Digest.[138]

The tone of the magazine was extremely critical of the clergy of the period. The articles and essays were frequently sarcastic and iconoclastic. Its positive message continued to be the urging of a return to these happy conditions (first-century unity), which alone would make possible the unity of Christ's followers, the purification of His church, and the triumph of the kingdom. But this required clearing away the accumulated corruptions of the centuries. The duty of destruction could not be evaded if there was to be building upon a solid foundation. So, Mr. Campbell became the iconoclast. "Restoration of the Ancient Order of Things" became the slogan, and it was applied with remorseless vigor. Whatever practice of the church was not validated by specific apostolic mandate must be discarded.[139] The work demanded positively "to develop from the New Testament a complete system of 'doctrine, worship, discipline, and government.' Negatively, it 'detected and exposed the various anti-Christian enormities, innovations, and corruptions which infect the Christian church.'"[140]

There were two stated goals in the Postscript to the *Declaration* and *Address*. The paper principally opposed the "pretensions of the clergy," "unauthorized organizations of the churches," and "the use of creeds as standards of orthodoxy or tests of fellowship." This meant no "missionary societies," "organs in public worship," titles such as "Reverend," "unimmersed" in fellowship. "It is not enough," Campbell taught, "that it is not forbidden—it is not commanded."[141] Here we see the emphasis on "silence."

---

138  *The Christian Baptist*, Alexander Campbell, February 7, 1825.
139  McAlister/DeGroot, p. 175.
140  *Ibid.*, p. 176.
141  *Ibid.*, p. 176.

## The Millennial Harbinger

Before *The Christian Baptist* ceased publication in July 1830, Campbell had launched in January of that year a new paper entitled *The Millennial Harbinger*, which was edited by him until January 1864 and by W. K. Pendleton, his son-in-law, until it ceased publication in 1870. The avowed purpose of the new periodical, as with *The Christian Baptist* was "the destruction of Sectarianism, Infidelity, and the Antichristian doctrine and practice,"[142] but the tone was decidedly more irenic and less iconoclastic. Its influence is beyond the scope of this chapter and will be considered in a study of "Innovations and Change."

## The Christian System

By January of 1835 Campbell had finished writing a systematic study of the scriptures under the title—*The Christian System*. The book began with a consideration of the universe, and Bible interpretation, and moved on to the nature of God and man, sin, the atonement, faith, repentance, baptism, conversion, the gift of the Holy Spirit, the Christian hope, the church, the ministry, and Christian discipline. In the section on Christian union, the Bible alone is shown to be the norm by which all doctrine, ordinances, polity, and piety are to be judged. Three lengthy treatises on the kingdom of heaven, remission of sins, and regeneration are included, because these seemed to be the areas in which discussion was most crucial.[143] The book was never very popular, influential, or significant in Restoration history and will occupy no more of our attention.

# Conclusion

We are by no means finished with the influence of Alexander Campbell on the Restoration Movement. It was in the *Millennial Harbinger* that he began to call for a "more efficient" organization through which to accomplish the church's mission to preach the gospel to the world. We will return to a discussion of his influence in conceiving and bringing forth the *American Christian Missionary Society*.

We have reached the point in this history where the work of Walter Scott is crucial, and we must stop to look at the impact that he made in spurring the "growth" of the movement and the "separation" of the movement from Baptist ties.

---

142  *Ibid.*, p. 176.
143  Murch, p. 138.

The influences of Alexander Campbell by 1830 were numerous, but chiefly he gave specific definition and application of his father's *Declaration* and *Address* and the motto—"Where the scriptures speak, we speak; where the scriptures are silent, we are silent." He will later raise an issue that will test the meaning of this slogan. We leave that for another time.

## Discussion

1. What publication announced the principles of restoration and unity? What periodical defined specifically the nature of these concepts? How would you compare the dispositions of Thomas and Alexander Campbell? What three abilities highlighted the talent and work of Alexander Campbell? What phrase describes Alexander's view of this movement?

2. When are where was Alexander Campbell born? Briefly describe his home life. Where did he receive his early education? How well did he do as a student? Where did he finish his education? How did this come about? Who influenced him at Glasgow? When did Alexander arrive in America? What did he read upon his arrival that made a strong impression on him? What did Alexander do before he began to preach?

3. What did Alexander first do as an indication of his controversial nature? What did the Christian Association become May 4, 1811? What issue was soon raised among its members? What conclusions were reached about baptism? What association did the Brush Run Church join with some reservations? What controversial sermon did Alexander preach before the Redstone Association in 1816?

4. What was Alexander's first effort to further the views of restoration? How long did it last? What, beginning in 1820, proved to be a successful means of propagation? What did the Walker and Maccalla debates discuss? The Owen debate? The Purcell debate? The Rice debate? What publication became the principal means of propagating restoration ideas? What was the tone of this paper? Give examples of some issues discussed in *The Christian Baptist*. Name two other publications that further set forth Alexander's views.

5. What did Campbell call for in *The Millennial Harbinger* that introduced a later controversy? What associate of Alexander spurred "growth" and "change" in the movement? How would you summarize Alexander's contribution to the restoration movement?

# Chapter 8

# The New Evangelism: Walter Scott

## Introduction

Walter Scott—not Sir Walter Scott the famous novelist and poet—take a place alongside Thomas Campbell, Alexander Campbell, and Barton W. Stone as one of, what some will call, the "four horsemen" of the Restoration Movement. Scott is credited with giving evangelistic zeal to the movement and with creating a clear line of demarcation between the "reformers" and the "Baptists"—two factors that kept the movement alive as a distinct body of Christians. "It was he," Garrison and DeGroot say, "who formulated and put into practice the effective evangelism method which had been lacking and it was who gave the impetus which changed a movement for reform within the Baptist churches into a separate religious body."[144]

Walter Scott was the youngest of the four men who are generally credited with laying the foundations of the Restoration Movement in America. He came out a similar background as Alexander Campbell and the two became close friends. They served as a complement to each other in that Campbell furnished the intellectual and theological guidance; and Scott, the practical evangelistic promotion necessary to any religious movement. It is often said that without the ministry of Walter Scott the work of the Campbells might have soon been forgotten.[145]

We, after looking at Scott's background and influences, want to look at his so-called "new-evangelism" and its impact on the relationship between the "Reformers" and the "Baptists."

## Walter Scott: Background and Early Influences

Walter Scott was born in Moffatt, Scotland, October 31, 1796. He studied at the University of Edinburgh. It is thought he obtained a degree, but because his name was so common in Scotland, it is impossible to identify him with

---

144 Garrison/DeGroot, p. 180. See also *Journey of Faith*, Lester G. McAllister and William Tucker, p. 133.
145 Murch, p. 97.

certainty in the university's records. Scott died at 64 on April 23, 1861. At the insistence of an uncle in New York, Scott came to America in 1818, where he spent the first year instructing Latin in an academy on Long Island. In 1819 he decided to move west and arrived in Pittsburgh on May 7, where he became an instructor in a school run by a fellow Scottish man, George Forrester. Forrester was the leader of a small church of humble, pious people, consisting of most Scotch and Irish.[146]

The church was one of several "primitive Christianity" congregations that had sprung up under the influence of Sandeman and the Haldanes. (See chapter 2, *Early British Movements*, for a review of Sandeman and the Haldanes.) Although this church in Pittsburgh practiced "foot washing" and the "holy kiss," it was devoted to the concept of restoration. Scott, who had been reared in the Church of Scotland, was impressed by Mr. Forrester's piety and by his passionate devotion to the direct study of the Bible as the source of religious truth. He became a member of this church.[147] After Forrester's death Scott had access to his library where he now could reference the important theological works of Haldane, Glas, and Sandeman.[148] While in the process of assimilating all these ideas (in the midst of running the academy and leading the church after Forrester died), Scott found a pamphlet written by Henry Errett, father of Isaac Errett, and published by a New York congregation of "Scotch Baptists" (the name generally given to the immersionist branch of the Sandemanians), who held many of the views taught by the Haldanes.

This tract focused on the purpose and effect of baptism. It connected baptism so definitely with the remission of sin and salvation that, in his view, it became highly questionable whether any of the unimmersed, regardless of the apparent possessions of the Spirit, could be "acknowledged as disciples, as having made the Christian profession, as having put on Christ, as having passed from death to life."[149] In the tract, Errett made the following conclusion:

> If the language employed respecting it, in many of the passages were to be taken literally, it would import, that remission of sins is to be obtained by baptism, that an escape from the wrath to come is effected in baptism; that men are born the children of God by baptism; that salvation is connected with baptism; that men wash

---

146 Garrison/DeGroot, p. 180.
147 *Ibid.*, p. 181.
148 Life of Elder Walter Scott, William Baxter, p. 61.
149 Garrison/DeGroot, p. 181.

away their sins by baptism; that men become dead to sin and alive to God by baptism; that the Church of God is sanctified and cleansed by baptism; that men are regenerated by baptism; and that the answer of a good conscience is obtained by baptism. All these things, if all the passages before us were construed literally, would be ascribed to baptism. And it was literal construction of these passages which led professed Christians, in the early ages, to believe that baptism was necessary to salvation. These conclusions are reached after citing the verses that substantiate each of the above points.[150]

Scott was so stirred by this discovery that he closed his school and traveled to New York where he sought to gain more instruction from the church that published this tract. Scott was soon disappointed in what he found in this church and several similar ones he visited in that area. He returned to Pittsburgh where once again he began to tutor. Scott now began rigorous study of the questions that Forrester had aroused. Locke, Glas, Sandeman, and Haldane were still among his favorite authors, but the Bible was his basic material.

## Walter Scott: Gospel Restored and New Evangelism

Walter Scott first met Alexander Campbell over the winter of 1821–22. The friendship that began during that time would have a profound effect on the Restoration Movement. From the time of his first meeting with Mr. Scott, Campbell felt he had met with no ordinary man, and having discovered, he was not slow to acknowledge his ability, and urged him to set forth his views in *The Christian Baptist*. Scott's first article appeared in the second issue and was entitled, "On Teaching Christianity." Scott continued this series in three later issues.

In these articles Scott argued that instead of trying to arouse an emotional state through what was called an "assurance of pardon," or "assurance that Christ died for me," with vivid pictures of the fate of the damned and wrestlings to win miraculous action of the Holy Spirit to bestow saving faith on a mourner already convicted of sin, it was better to try to produce belief in the Messiahship of Jesus by presenting evidence.[151] Scott's emphasis, as his

---

150 Baxter, p. 47–51. These pages contain a number of excerpts from Errett's tract.
151 Garrison/DeGroot, p. 184.

biographer indicates, was moving in the direction of restoring the "gospel" more than restoring the "order" of the church.

> "Up to this time nearly all the efforts made by these advocates for reform were confined to the correcting of evils and abuses in the church, and comparatively little was done for the conversion of sinners; and the result, of course, was, that while many were led to adopt the views set forth with zeal and vigor, there was but little growth in the churches as far as numbers were concerned. They had not, as yet clearly perceived the distinction between the *original order of the church* and the *original gospel* and were so occupied with an attempt to reform the church and unite the various conflicting parties, that they did not perceive that there was an equal necessity for urging the original pleas, as made by the apostles in their address to the world. The necessity of going before the world with the gospel message of entreaty and invitation soon became apparent in the mind of Scott."[152]

## *Scott/Mahoning Association*

After considerable criticism and objections, the "Reformers," converts among the Campbells, left the conservative Redstone Association of Baptists to join the more liberal and less critical Mahoning Association of Baptists in 1824. Here they were given greater freedom to express their views of restoration.

In the summer of 1826 Scott moved to Steubenville, Ohio and opened an academy. At this time, he was not part of the "Reformers" or the Mahoning Association. At the time of his arrival, he described the state of the churches there:

> There were three parties struggling to restore original Christianity; the first of them calling themselves "the Churches of Christ,"; the second calling themselves "Christians," (Stone's group, LAS); and the third laying at that time chiefly in the bosom of the Regular Baptist Churches and originating with the writings and labors of Bro. A Campbell. To the first of these parties, up to 1826, belonged your humble servant, Walter Scott.[153]

In the summer of 1826, the Mahoning Baptist Association held its annual meeting nearby and Scott attended. Although not a member, he was by

---

152 Baxter, p. 80–81.
153 *The Evangelist*, Walter Scott, editor. April 1, 1833, p. 93.

courtesy invited to participate as a "teaching brother." On Sunday he delivered the morning sermon based on Matthew 11 and made a deep impression on the hearers. Alexander Campbell was present and was much impressed by Scott's eloquence and the finished nature of his address.[154]

Growth among the "Reformers" was minimal by 1827 and the Mahoning Association was concerned over the lack of response. "The Mahoning Association in 1827 listed seventeen churches. Fourteen of them were represented at the meeting. The reports for the year were not encouraging. There had been a total of thirty-four baptisms and thirteen additions otherwise. Thirteen had been excommunicated. The net gain was sixteen— and this at a time when the population was doubling and redoubling. The association decided it needed an evangelist "to labor among the churches." [155] It appointed a committee to find the man, who nominated Walter Scott and was elected by the Association.

## *New Evangelism*

Scott developed a simple and "novel" style of preaching that caught on among other preachers and brought immediate results with hundreds of responses. "When the Mahoning Association held its next annual meeting, August 1828, the churches reported a net increase of 512 for the year. The moderator, Stephen Wood, added that 'these, however, are but the half of the actual number, which have been by our means immersed into the Lord Jesus during the last year.'"[156] By 1829, another thousand converts had been added to the congregations.

Scott's novel method was his five-finger way of showing the relationship and sequence of faith, repentance, baptism, forgiveness, and the gift of the Holy Spirit. "His mind was analytical, and he so simplified a subject that all could understand. He told the people that the gospel, in general, was threefold: facts, commands, and promises. The facts were to be believed, the commands to be obeyed, and the promises to be enjoyed."

But in its specific application, it was fivefold:

1. Faith to change the heart.
2. Repentance to change the life.
3. Baptism to change the state.
4. Remission of sins to cleanse the guilt.

---

154 Murch, p. 100.
155 Garrison/DeGroot, p. 186–87.
156 *Ibid.*, p. 189.

5. The gift of the Holy Spirit to help in the religious life and make one a partake of the divine nature.[157]

"It is said that one of Scott's favorite methods of announcing his meetings was to go to the schoolhouse and after dismissal meet the children. He would introduce himself and ask if they would like to learn a new five-finger exercise. Thereupon he would say, 'Lift your left hand. Now beginning with your thumb repeat after me: Faith, repentance, baptism, remission of sins, gift of the Holy Spirit. Now again, faster, altogether.' After the drill, he would advise the children to go home, repeat this to their parents and tell them that the man who taught them would be preaching that night and all were invited. Immediately the whole neighborhood would be alerted, and the meeting place filled to overflowing on the first night."[158]

Thomas Campbell learned of Scott's method, decided to visit one of his services, and felt that for the first time he was hearing the gospel preached in a new and practical way. Said Campbell, "We have long known the former (theory), and have spoken and published many things correctly concerning the ancient gospel, its simplicity and perfect adaptation to the present state of mankind, for the benign and gracious purposes of his immediate relief and complete salvation; but I must confess that, in respect to the *direct exhibition* and *application* of it for that blessed purpose, I am at present for the first time upon the ground where the thing has appeared to be *practically exhibited* to the proper purpose."[159]

## *The Gospel Restored*

Although Scott granted that the Campbells had done much to restore the order of the church, he firmly believed that this "new evangelism" was the beginning of the restoration of the ancient gospel. Scott published a monthly periodical, *The Evangelist,* from 1832–1842, but in place of the paper in 1836 he published a book—*The Gospel Restored, A Discourse.* He subtitled it more fully, *A Discourse of the True Gospel.* His analysis of the restoration movement, as stated in the preface includes, "First the Bible was adopted as sole authority in our assemblies, to the exclusion of all other books. Next the Apostolic order was proposed. Finally, the True Gospel was restored."[160] The first of these he would attribute to many men, the second to Alexander Campbell, and the last to himself.

---

157 The Restoration Movement of the Nineteenth Century, M. M. Davis, p. 164.
158 Much, p. 102–03.
159 Garrison/DeGroot, p. 189.
160 p. v, vi.

It was certainly Scott's idea that it was he who had first preached the true gospel of salvation from sin in its original form. "Scott began his work at New Lisbon, Ohio. The first convert under his new way of presenting the ancient gospel was William Amend, of whom Scott's early biographer, Baxter, says that he was 'beyond all question, the first person in modern times who received the ordinance of baptism in perfect accordance with apostolic teaching and usage'. This was on November 18, 1827."[161]

## Walter Scott: Mahoning Association and Dissolution

By 1830 the success of Scott's evangelism, which was clearly not "Baptist," had radically changed the churches in northeastern Ohio, the home of the Mahoning Baptist Association. There was only one thing left to do which was to remove the last trace of its distinctively Baptist character; that was for the association itself to be dissolved. It did so at Austintown, OH in August 1830.

The dissolution happened most likely at Scott's instigation, and certainly with his support. John Henry introduced a resolution that "the Mahoning Association, as an advisory council, or an ecclesiastical tribunal, should cease to exist."[162] Alexander Campbell, who was rising to oppose the notion, was dissuaded by Scott. It was adopted unanimously. What happened in Austintown was only the beginning of dissolutions among many Baptist associations which were dominated by the "Reformers." Other Baptist associations began pronouncing anathemas against the "Reformers" and listing syllabuses of errors charged against them.

For example, the Beaver Association of western Pennsylvania had anathematized the Mahoning Association the year before it was dissolved, charging the "Reformers" with teaching:

> That there is no promise of salvation without baptism; that baptism should be administered on belief that Jesus Christ is the Son of God, without examination on any other point; that there is no direct operation of the Holy Spirit on the mind before baptism; that baptism procures the remission of sins and the gift of the Holy Spirit; that man's obedience place it in God's power to elect to salvation; that no creed is necessary for the church; that

---

161 Garrison/DeGroot, p. 187; see Baxter, p. 103–108.
162 *Ibid.*, p.103–108.

all baptized persons have a right to administer the ordinance of baptism.[163]

To these items, Tate's Creek Association added four more Campbellite errors:

1. That there is no special call to the ministry.
2. That the law given to Moses is abolished.
3. That experimental religion is enthusiasm.
4. That there is no mystery in the Scriptures.[164]

The process of separation was well advanced by the end of 1830. By 1833, the separation was virtually complete. "At that time and place, in Austintown, OH, in August 1830, there came into being a company of Reformers who were not Baptists. 'Those Baptists who had embraced the new views,' says Baxter, 'together with the new converts made, were called Campbellites and by many Scotties, but after the dissolution of the association which was really brought about by the efforts of Scott, they were called 'Disciples.'"[165]

Scott regarded the dissolution of the Mahoning Association as "the wisest course and assumed whatever responsibly there might be in the matter." He believed that it "really made those who had accepted the primitive gospel a new and distinct people and that it freed the Disciples from the last vestige of human authority, and placed them under Christ, with His word for their guide.[166]

## Conclusion

Alexander Campbell in *The Christian Baptist* from 1823–1830 set a negative, iconoclastic tone by fighting sectarianism, the clergy, human creeds, etc. to restore the ancient order of things. Scott saw in this negative approach a neglect of the "ancient gospel"—the apostolic appeal and invitation to sinners by the positive, simple evangelism of faith, repentance, baptism, remission of sins, and the gift of the Holy Spirit.

Scott, affectionately referred to as the "silver-tongued orator" and the "golden oracle" of the Restoration Movement moved sinners to obedience, restored a simple form of evangelism that brought immediate growth and enduring expansion to the movement. This growth by the simple New Testament mode of evangelism alienated Baptists and established distinctive

---

163 Garrison/DeGroot, p. 194.
164 *Ibid.*, p. 194.
165 *Ibid.*, p. 192. See Baxter, p. 217.
166 Baxter, p. 217–18.

bodies of believers that moved along different and separate lines from the Baptists. Scott recognized the distinct and different groups seeking to restore the ancient order and gospel. It remained in 1830 for these diverse groups to themselves to be united as one. That we will look at in the next chapter.

## Discussion

1. Who were the four horsemen of the Restoration Movement? What did Scott give to the movement? What change did he help make in the movement? How would you compare Scott and Campbell?

2. Where was Scott born? When? Where was he educated? When did he come to America? What did he do? Where did he soon move? Who did he meet in Pittsburgh? What kind of church did he find? What important reading did he do? Whose tract did he read? What did it emphasize? How did Scott react? Who did he meet in the winter of 1821–22?

3. What was Campbell's estimate of Scott? What did Scott emphasize as opposed to Campbell? What Baptist Association did the Reformers join in 1824? Why? How many parties did Scott see working toward restoration? What did he call them? What did Campbell think of Scott as a preacher? What was bothering the Mahoning Association in 1827? What did they do about it? Describe Scott's "novel" way of preaching? What effect did it have on growth? What did Thomas Campbell think of Scott's preaching? What did Scott think his preaching had restored? Who was his first convert?

4. What happened to the Mahoning Association as a result of Scott's type of preaching? What did he influence the association to do? How did antagonistic Baptists react? What were some differences they anathematized? When was the separation from the Baptists complete? What did separation make the Disciples?

5. What was Campbell's approach to restoration? What was Scott's approach? What two things did Scott's approach produce? What work must now be done?

# Chapter 9

# The Merging of the Two Groups

## Introduction

By 1830 distinct bodies of "Christians" and "Disciples" in the states of Kentucky, Ohio, Illinois, Indiana, Tennessee, etc., often existed side by side in the same communities. The similarity of their views and their common goals of unity would in time naturally lend themselves to a plea for fellowship and unity between the two groups. The years of 1831–32 mark the fullness of time for this idea—a time when, after much writing on the topic in the *Christian Messenger* (Barton W. Stone) and the *Millennial Harbinger* (Alexander Campbell), several independent but simultaneous efforts successfully united groups of "Christians" and "Disciples." Although many local figures made these mergers possible, the story of unions centers on and primarily revolves around the work of four men: Barton W. Stone, John T. Johnson, "Raccoon" John Smith, and John Rogers.

## Unity: The Time Had Come

Within their first decade, the most important event in the history of the Disciples was the union between the Reformers (Disciples, LAS), who had responded to the call of the Campbells and Scott, and the western "Christians," among whom Barton W. Stone had been the most influential figure, especially since he began editing *The Christian Messenger* in 1826. At the time, the two major groups of New Testament Christians were the Reformers or Disciples, under the leadership of the Campbells and Scott, and the Christians, under Stone. It is variously estimated that each group numbered from eight to ten thousand members.[167]

Previously we noted that the Reformers dissolved their relationship with the Baptists in 1830. It has been said that the Baptist-Reformer split opened the way for the Disciples and Christians to consider the possibility of uniting. Both groups had their greatest visibility and numerical strength in the same general area of the country—particularly in the Kentucky-Ohio region.

---
167  Much, p. 110.

Forced to withdraw from the Baptists, Disciples formed congregations in many communities that already had a congregation of Christians.[168]

As the two groups became acquainted with each other, they came to see that they shared such in common. Both groups advocated Christian primitivism and affirmed the necessity of uniting the church to proclaim the Christian message with integrity and force. Both groups accepted the principle of unity in essentials, liberty in nonessentials, and charity in all things. Both groups rejected creeds as tests of Christian fellowship and the authority of church bodies which usurped the prerogatives of local congregations. Both recognized but two ordinances, the Lord's Supper, and baptism, and practiced believers' baptism by immersion. Both opposed sectarian and unscriptural names.[169]

Any unity or merging of congregations would happen one by one in each community where two groups met separately. As Garrison says, "Since the churches of both groups exercised a high degree of local independence, union could not have been brought about by any binding act of conferences or conventions…it had to depend upon a contagion of fellowship between their congregations in many communities."[170] They, as we soon shall see, had a place to accomplish this.

As early as 1828 this contagion and fellowship was developing as congregations of Christians and Disciples were corresponding with one another, conferring with one another, opening their meetinghouses and pulpits to one another, and agreeing to mingle with one another.[171]

# Unity:
# The Men of the Hour

Stone had opened his paper, *The Christian Messenger* to a discussion and promotion of merger between the two groups. "Replying to a correspondent who asked why the Christians should not unite with the 'New Testament Baptists' (Campbell's Reformers), Stone wrote in 1828: 'If there is a difference between us, we know it not. We have nothing in us to prevent a union; and if they have nothing in them in opposition to it, we are in spirit one. May God strengthen the cords of Christian union.'"[172]

---

168  McAlister/Tucker, p. 147.
169  *Ibid.*, p. 147.
170  *An American Religious Movement,* Winfred Ernest Garrison, p. 90.
171  McAlister/Tucker, p. 149–50.
172  Garrison, p. 95.

Alexander Campbell, who began publishing *The Millennial Harbinger* in 1830, was not a prime mover in these early efforts for union, but something must be said about his reaction to what became a reality in 1831. He and Stone had some serious differences over who first restored the ancient order, and over the trinity and nature of Christ, the atonement, the name, baptism, etc. In the latter part of 1831 Campbell and Stone engaged in an extended and sometimes heated exchange about uniting Christians and Disciples. If the union of Christians and Disciples had depended solely upon the goodwill between Campbell and Stone, it never would have been accomplished.[173] After much correspondence Campbell was now wary of Stone. "He had heard too much about Stone's theological speculations and about some practices of the Christians 'which had gone past Jerusalem after departing from Babylon.' He said he would be honored by a merger with the 'larger' and 'respectable' Christian denominations, but he would refuse it if it meant in any way the submerging of 'the ancient gospel and the ancient order of things.'"[174] Campbell's priority, as in *The Christian Baptist*, was "restoration" then "unity."

When Campbell heard of the union at Lexington, KY and the right hand of fellowship extended between Stone (Christian) and "Raccoon" John Smith (Disciple) he responded rather sharply: "These brethren need not to be told that to convert persons is not merely to baptize them, to loose them and let them go; nor to give them the name Christian, and induce them to protest against human leaders, against human creeds, and to extol the sufficiency of the inspired writings; but 'to turn them from darkness to light, and from the power of Satan to God, that they may receive forgiveness of sins and an inheritance amongst them that are sanctified—*to teach them to observe and do all that the Lord commanded.*'"[175]

## John T. Johnson

A Baptist until February 1831, John T. Johnson accepted Alexander Campbell's views at that time, left the Baptist church and organized a congregation on Reform principles. Thereafter he abandoned law and politics and gave his entire energy to the promotion of the movement. As a close friend and neighbor to Stone he came into sympathetic cooperation with the Christians and was regarded by them as one of themselves. Perhaps

---

173  McAlister/Tucker, p. 150.
174  Murch, p.113.
175  *Ibid.*, p. 113–14.

more than any other one man he became the personal link between the two parties.[176]

### John Smith and John Rogers

After several mergers, especially the one at Lexington, KY, "Raccoon" John Smith and John Rogers were sent out to proclaim the merger to other churches and urge them to take up the cause of unity. "To increase and consolidate this union, and to convince all our sincerity, we, the Elders and brethren, have separated Elders, John Smith and John Rogers, the first known *formerly* by the name of Reformer, the latter by the name of Christian. These brethren are to ride together and through all the churches, and to be equally supported by the united contributions of the churches of both descriptions, which contributions are to be deposited together, with Brother John T. Johnson as treasurer and distributor."[177]

# Unity:
# The Right Hand of Fellowship

### Millersburg, KY

"Christians and Disciples in Millersburg, KY united on April 24, 1831. According to the record book of the Millersburg Christian Church: 'It was the practice of the brethren forming the two congregations to commune together at their several meetings, and finally finding themselves to be one so far as faith and practice were concerned, they agreed to meet without regard to differences of opinion, acknowledging no name but that of Christian, and no creed but the Bible.' The result of these joint meetings was a union into one congregation in the year of 1831, at which meeting they pledged themselves to each other not to indulge in speculations to the wounding of each other, but regard to the gospel as the power of God for salvation to all who believe and obey it."[178]

### Georgetown, KY

"Providentially the Great Crossings Church, shepherded by John T. Johnson, a Reformer, and the Georgetown church, served by Barton W. Stone, were within a stone's throw of one another, and the two men had a common

---

176  Garrison/DeGroot, p. 213. Also, see *Life of Elder John Smith,* John Augustus Williams, p. 367–68.
177  Williams, p. 376, 378.
178  McAlister/Tucker, p. 150.

passion for Christian unity. Their abilities and leadership were widely recognized among the two bodies of Christians. In solemn prayer and pledge they agreed to promote national union.

When "Raccoon" John Smith, another Reformer preacher of great power, was invited by Johnson to hold a meeting at Great Crossing in November 1831, a conference developed between the three preachers and one of Stone's warmest co-laborers, John Rogers. They agreed to announce their plan of union to their respective congregations and see if they approved if it. Finding almost unanimous approval, the four men determined to write and preach for Christian union. Stone, Johnson, Rogers, and Smith arranged dates and places for joint meetings of Christians and Reformers. Usually, three or four days were spent in each community. Christmas 1831, coming on the Lord's Day, they decided they would celebrate Christ's birthday and the birth of the new year by a festival of unity. For Georgetown the meeting would be December 23–26.[179]

## **Lexington, KY**

The Georgetown unity meeting was followed by a larger one at the Hill St. Church in Lexington on January 1, 1832. There, the chief spokesmen were Stone and Smith. Conscious of the solemnity and importance of the occasion, Smith stressed the need to speak on controversial subjects "in the words which the Lord has given," to eliminate the binding of human opinions, and to stand on the Bible alone. He then concluded, "Let us, then, brethren, be no longer Campbellites or Stoneites, New Lights or Old Lights, or any other kind of *lights*, but let us all come to the Bible and the Bible alone, as the only book in the world that can give us all the Light we need."[180]

Stone arose, his heart glowing with love, and every pulse bounding with hope. "I will not attempt," said he, "to introduce any new topic, but will say a few things on the same subjects already presented by my beloved brother… I have not one objection to the ground laid down by him as the true scriptural basis of union among the people of God; and I am willing to give him, now and here, my hand." He then turned as he spoke and offered to Smith a hand trembling with rapture and brotherly love, and it was grasped by a hand full of the honest pledges of fellowship, and the union was virtually accomplished.[181]

---

179   Murch, p. 110–11.
180   Williams, p. 371–73.
181   *Ibid.*, p. 373.

## *Other Unions*

Several mergers transpired about the time of the Georgetown-Lexington meetings; others occurred much later over the next two-three years.

### Indiana

On December 24, 1831, John Longley, a Christian from Rush County, IN (the home of John P. Thompson) writing to Elder Stone, said, "The Reforming Baptists (Campbells, LAS) and we are all one here."[182]

### Tennessee

Griffith Cathey, of Tennessee, on January 4, 1832, wrote:

> The members of the Church of Christ, and the members known by the name Disciples or Reformed Baptists, regardless of all charges about Trinitarianism, Arianism, and Socinianism, and of the questions whether it is possible for any person to get to heaven without immersion is for the remission of sins, have come forward, given the right hand of fellowship, and united upon the plain and simple gospel.[183]

## *Opposition*

This above report from Tennessee implies the presence of differences and disputes. As already noted, Campbell and Stone had sharp disagreements over several issues, and it was these differences that created considerable opposition to the mergers.

### Differences

Without detailing all the differences, it is important to have a sense of the areas of dispute. Campbell and Stone disputed over the name—whether to wear the name "Christian" or "Disciple." Stone thought Disciples were Calvinistic in the "substitutionary" view of the atonement. Some charged Stone with being as an Arian because of his view of the nature of Christ. Stone was more tolerant and received into membership those who had only been sprinkled; Stone emphasized unity at the expense of restoration and Campbell stressed restoration in precedence over unity. Disciples observed the Lord's Supper weekly and the Christians less frequently. Christians

---

182  *Ibid.*, p. 373.
183  *Ibid.*, p. 375.

were less 'anticlerical' than the Disciples who fought all signs of an ordained ministry.[184]

An example of the difficulties and opposition is the Hill Street Church in Lexington, KY where Stone and Smith gave each other the right hand of fellowship. The church had differences over the necessity of having ordained ministers. "Many of the Christians held the opinion that none but Elders or Preachers could lawfully or properly administer the ordinances, while the Disciples denied the exclusive privilege of the clergy in this matter. Under the circumstances, therefore, many felt unprepared to go into the proposed union. After due reflection and conference, a meeting was held on February 25, and the pledge of union was dissolved, and each party stood on its former ground. Nor was a union between the two congregations finally and formally effected until July 1835.[185]

"Raccoon" John Smith, a Reformer, in his travels throughout Kentucky to promote mergers, ran into considerable opposition among the Reformers over the views of Barton W. Stone that dominated the thinking of the Christians. Williams, in his biography of Smith, publishes an address by Smith that was used to settle the minds of the Reformers about Stone's views. The address seeks to allay fears over Stone's view of the atonement, receiving the unimmersed, the nature of Christ, eating the Lord's Supper with those who accepted Stone's views, and the neglect of complete restoration.[186]

# Conclusion

From 1832 onward, mergers continued to occur. By 1835, "the greater part of the Christian churches in the areas mentioned had joined the merger. On the points of difference, especially baptism and evangelistic method, the practice of Campbell and Scott prevailed. The Christians contributed a revived emphasis upon liberty of opinion and upon union, which the Reformers had been in danger of subordinating in their zeal for the restoration of 'a particular ecclesiastical order.'"[187]

A period of expansion and growth followed these mergers and by 1860 the 20,000 or so Christians at the beginning of the union meetings had grown, by fairly accurate count to 200,000. At the very time unity was developing and the movement was expanding, new thinking and new ideas were arising

---

184  McAlister/Tucker, p. 148–49; Murch, p. 114–118.
185  Williams, p. 377–78.
186  *Ibid.*, p. 382–87.
187  Garrison, p. 99.

that contained seeds of discord. The sowing of those seeds will be the topic in the next chapter.

## Discussion

1. What distinct groups existed by 1830? What did they notice about their views and goals? What did these groups begin to do by 1831–32? What four men were especially committed to this work?

2. Who was most influential among the Christians? How many Christians and Disciples were there by 1830? What circumstance seems to call for mergers? What were some of their similarities? How would this fellowship or merger have to come about? What were the two groups doing by 1828?

3. Who was a prime mover in this through *The Christian Messenger*? Who had considerable reservations about the merger? What differences did Campbell and Stone have? Who was the "personal link" between the two groups? What two men travelled to encourage the merger?

4. Where did the first merger occur? Where did the four principal men meet to discuss merger? When did the Georgetown meeting take place? What church in Lexington opened the new year with a unity meeting? Who spoke first at Lexington? How did Stone respond? Where did other unions occur? List differences that threatened unity. When did Lexington finally unite? Who addressed these differences in Kentucky?

# Chapter 10

# Innovations and Change

## Introduction

The "new" evangelism initiated by Walter Scott brought sudden growth to the Restoration Movement along with an intense desire to organize the movement for greater efficiency in promoting the cause. It also created a desire to keep up with the denominations by enhancing worship with mechanical instruments.

The establishment of the missionary society marked the climax of years of intense effort on the part of Alexander Campbell to urge the brotherhood to establish some kind of general organization through which the entire brotherhood could cooperate to evangelize the world.[188]

In 1851 a brother wrote J. B. Henshall, associate editor of the *Ecclesiastical Reformer*:

> What say you of instrumental music in our churches? Should not the Christian Church have organs or Bass Viols that the great object of Psalmody might be consummated? Would not such instruments add greatly to the solemnity of worship, and cause the hearts of the saints to be raised to a higher state of devotion while the deep toned organ would swell its notes of "awful sound"? I think it is high time we awaken to the importance of this subject. We are far in the rear of Protestants on the subject of church music. I hope, therefore, that you will give your views in extenso, on this much neglected subject.[189]

The call for innovations and change in organization and worship raised new and important questions about authority and the meaning of Thomas Campbell's slogan—where the scriptures speak, we speak; where the scriptures are silent, we are silent.

Although the missionary society and mechanical instruments demand an examination of the meaning and scripturalness of Campbell's slogan, we must first look at the two issues as they evolved historically—our study for this chapter.

---

188 West, Vol. 1, p. 166.
189 *Ibid.*, p. 308–09.

# Growth and Evangelism: The Demands for Greater Efficiency

By the influence of Walter Scott, as previously noted, the Restoration movement experienced extensive and sudden growth. From 1827–1828 the movement by 1000, as it did also between 1828–1829. By the beginning of 1860, there were as many as 200,000 members. "The impulse to evangelize was the primary cause of cooperation. Disciples in and around New Lisbon, Ohio met there in 1831 to devise some cooperative plan for spreading the gospel, and an organization of churches by counties was proposed. In *The Christian Messenger* of August 1833, there is a letter from Thomas C. Johnson of Spencer, Indiana, announcing a three-day session at Union Meetinghouse (Gosport) for October. Its object, he said, was 'to converse and agree to cooperate in employing some useful brother laborer to perform the duties of evangelist'."[190]

Alexander Campbell also saw the possibilities of growth, changed his tactics, and issued a new paper, *The Millennial Harbinger*. In its pages Campbell envisioned the coming a new society through which the work of the Restoration movement—a society he thought of as the Millennial Kingdom. In the prospectus of his new paper, he states its purpose:

> This work shall be devoted to the destruction of sectarianism, infidelity, and anti-Christian doctrine and practice. It shall have for its object the development and introduction of that political and religious order of society called THE MILLENNIUM, which will be the consummation of that ultimate amelioration of society proposed in the Christian scriptures.[191]

Campbell had a decidedly different view of cooperation and organization when he began publishing *The Christian Baptist* in 1823. There and then he wrote:

> But every Christian who understands the nature and design, the excellence and glory, of the institution called the church of Jesus Christ, will lament to see its glory transferred to a human corporation. The church is robbed of its character by every institution, merely human, that would ape its excellence and substitute itself in its place.[192]

---

190 Garrison/DeGroot, p. 234–35.
191 Benjamin Lyon Smith, *The Millennial Harbinger Abridged*, Vol. 1, p. XV.
192 The Christian Baptist, Vol. 1, p. 33.

In May 1831 Campbell began a series of five essays in *The Millennial Harbinger* about cooperation and organized work. In the absence of Campbell, the second and third articles were written by Walter Scott but do not materially change the viewpoint that was the logical forerunner of state and national organizations and societies. The essays thoroughly explored the theme of cooperation culminating in the proposition that were the task is too great for a local congregation, many congregations should go together to perform it. Campbell wrote: "A church can do what an individual disciple cannot, and so can a district of churches do what a single congregation cannot."[193]

The call by Campbell, along with others, for a greater cooperation and more efficient organization brought forth several state-wide organizations to promote evangelism. "Mr. Campbell became a leader and the principal defender of the movement toward county, district, state, and eventually national organization. Garrison/DeGroot detail a state organization as early as 1833 in Ohio, and others soon thereafter in Kentucky, Pennsylvania, Indiana, and other states."[194]

In February 1849 Campbell wrote in *The Millennial Harbinger*:

> There is now heard from the East and the West, from the North and the South, one general, if not universal, call for a more efficient organization of our churches. Experience, then which there is not a more sufficient teacher, decides and promulgates that our present cooperative system is comparatively inefficient and inadequate to the exigencies of the times and the cause we plead.[195]

The stage was now set for the organization of a national society for the propagation of the faith.

## National Organization: The American Christian Missionary Society

In 1842 Alexander Campbell began a series of articles on "Church Organization" in *The Millennial Harbinger* which ran until 1848. The first essay is in a sense the most important as it represents a charter for organizational development beyond the local congregation. In the article Campbell sets forth five arguments for organization, ending in a stated

---

193 McAlister/Tucker, p. 168–69.
194 Garrison/DeGroot, p. 236–42.
195 West, p. 167.

principle. His fifth article states: "We cannot concentrate the action of the tens of thousands of Israel, in any great Christian effort, but by cooperation." Campbell then concludes, "We can have no thorough cooperation without a more ample, extensive, and thorough church organization."[196]

The widespread discussion of church organization and Campbell's essays on the subject between 1845 and 1848 produced a desire for some sort of general structure through which all the churches could cooperate to evangelize the world. In the August 1849 issue of *The Millennial Harbinger* Campbell expressed his hopes and fears for the convention. He said:

> I am of the opinion that a Convention ... a Convention of messengers of churches, selected and constituted such by the churches—one from every church, if possible, or if impossible, one from a district, or some definite number of churches. It is not to be comprised of a few self-appointed messengers from one, two, or three districts, or States, but a general Convention.[197]

The first national Convention of Disciples was held at Cincinnati, October 23–28, 1849, which 156 delegates from 100 churches and 11 states. It assembled in the Christian Church at the corner of Fourth and Walnut Streets. Formal organization was the first order of business. Alexander Campbell, though absent, was elected president.[198]

W. K. Pendleton, Campbell's son-in-law, wrote after the convention his explanations of why they met:

> We met, not for the purpose of enacting ecclesiastical law, not to interfere with the true and scriptural independence of the churches, but to consult about the best ways for giving efficiency to our power, and to devise such methods of cooperation, in the great work of converting and sanctifying, as our combined counsels, under the guidance of Providence, might suggest and approve. There are some duties of the church which a single congregation cannot, by her unaided strength discharge. A primary object being to devise some scheme for a more effectual proclamation of the gospel in destitute places, both at home and abroad, the Convention took under consideration the organization of a Missionary Society.[199]

---

196  McAlister/Tucker, p. 170–71.
197  *Ibid.*, p. 174.
198  See West, p. 172 and Garrison/DeGroot, p. 245.
199  West, p. 173.

The delegates of the convention in Cincinnati approved of a constitution of 13 articles that detail the nature of the society. Several articles are presented to convey the make-up and character of the society.

1. Article 1: This society shall be called the American Christian Missionary Society.
2. Article 2: The object of this society shall be to promote the spread of the gospel in destitute places of our own and foreign lands.
3. Article 3: The Society shall be composed of annual delegates, Life Members and Life Directors. Any church may appoint a delegate for an annual contribution of ten dollars. Twenty dollars paid at one time will be requisite to constitute a member for life, and one hundred dollars paid at one time, or a sum which in addition to any previous contributions shall amount to one hundred dollars, shall be required to constitute a director for life.
4. Article 4: The officers of the Society shall consist of a president, twenty vice-presidents, a treasurer, a corresponding secretary, and a recording secretary, who shall be elected by the members of the Society at its annual meeting.
5. Article 5: The Society shall also annually elect twenty-five managers, who together with the officers and life directors of this Society, shall constitute an executive board, to conduct the business of the Society, and shall continue in office until their successors are elected, seven of whom shall constitute a quorum for the transaction of business.
6. Article 7: The executive board shall have power to appoint its own meetings, elect its own chairman, enact its own by-laws and rules of order, provided always that they be not inconsistent with the Constitution; fill such vacancies which may occur in their body, or in the offices of the Society during the year, and if deemed necessary by two-thirds of the members present at a regular meeting, convene special meetings of the Society. They shall establish such agencies as the interest of the Society may require, appoint agents and missionaries, fix their compensation, direct, and instruct them concerning their particular fields and labors, make all appropriations to be paid out of the treasury, and to present to the Society at each annual meeting a full report of their proceedings during the past year.
7. Article 10: All the officers, managers, missionaries, and agents of the Society, shall be members in good standing in the churches of God.
8. Article 11: The Society shall meet annually at Cincinnati on the first Wednesday after the third Lord's Day of October, or at such time and

place as shall have been designated at the previous meeting.
9. Article 13: No alteration of this constitution shall be made without a vote of two-thirds of the members present at an annual meeting, not unless the same shall have been proposed at a previous annual meeting or recommended by the executive board.

## *Opposition*

It should not be supposed that there was no immediate and serious opposition to the organization of this Society. A church in Connellsville, PA, Detroit, MI, and Virginia registered objections. The Connellsville church provides us with one such example:

> The church in Connellsville, Pennsylvania got to the heart of the issue with a letter stating 10 resolutions and containing lengthy comments about the resolutions. In essence the letter said, "That the Church of Jesus Christ, is, in its constitution and design essentially missionary, we conceive to be an axiomatic truth. Not a missionary society, but emphatically and preeminently *the* missionary society, the only one authorized by Jesus Christ; her constitu9ion the Holy Scriptures; the end for which she was established, the conversion and sanctification of the world. For this purpose, she is fully commissioned by her great Head, and fully qualified to fulfill that commission. To affirm that she is not competent is to charge her all-wise Founder with the inconsistency of assigning her to a duty which she is unable to perform. If then, she is authorized and competent, all other societies for this purpose are not only unscriptural, but they are unnecessary and uncalled for. Unscriptural, because they appropriate to themselves the duty and honor which belong to the church; unnecessary, because the end for which they are instituted the church is fully able to accomplish.[200]

Even though objections were raised by these congregations, Jacob Creath Jr., emerged as primary opponent in the early months following the establishment of the Missionary Society. His major objections will be covered in the next chapter. But for now, let us note Creath's challenge to Campbell which raises the issue of scriptural authority:

> You place conventions on a level with the church of God and civil governments. From the Acts of the Apostles, we have authority for

---
200 Hailey, p. 167.

the organization of all the early Christian churches. Paul says the governments that exist are ordained by God, Romans 13. Now, if you will produce as good authority for conventions as I have for the congregations of God and civil governments, *I will yield the controversy to you.*[201]

For several reasons which we will note later, opposition to the American Christian Missionary Society did not become substantial until the close of the Civil War in 1865. Those objections will be analyzed in the next chapter.

# Instrumental Music: The Search for Improved Worship

On February 22, 1851, the issue of instrumental music in worship was raised for the first time on record. As noted in the first part of this chapter, a letter to the *Ecclesiastical Reformer* urged the use of mechanical instruments to enhance the solemnity, devotion, majestic sounds of worship, and to keep up with the denominations who were beginning to use it.

The response by associate editor J. B. Henshall to the letter is typical about the feelings about "mechanical" worship:

> In proportion as men have become worldly minded, provided they have not entirely lost the fear of God, do they begin to require *helps* to their devotion. That they could require such helps under a dark dispensation where they were rather lead into the use of symbolic rites, than inwardly illuminated by God's word and spirit, is not at all astonishing; but to say that we need them who live in the full light of gospel privileges, and enjoy God's mercies and providence over us, is to say that we have no gratitude in our hearts, and that we are every way unworthy of these benefits.[202]

Mechanical instruments of music in worship were viewed as the desire of the carnal or animalistic man. Alexander Campbell in October 1851 concluded:

> So to those who have no real devotion or spirituality in them, and whose animal nature flags under the oppression of church service, I think with Mr. G., that instrumental music would be not only a desideratum (desire/need, LAS), but an essential prerequisite to fire up their souls to even animal devotion. But I presume, to all

---

201 West, p. 202.
202 *Ibid.*, p. 309.

spiritually minded Christians such aids would be as a cowbell in a concert.²⁰³

The issue of instruments of music in worship came up once more that same year in Millersburg, KY. Aylette Raines, in 1851, was preaching at Millersburg. Raines was in the habit of keeping a diary, and on April 27, 1851, made the following entry: "Brother Saunders wishes to introduce the melodeon into the church."²⁰⁴ Raines, however, bitterly opposed it, and it did not get in at Millersburg at this time. The subject of instrumental music did not come up again before the brotherhood until 1860. At this time, a letter was sent to Ben Franklin (not the statesman, LAS), asking him to express his views on the use of the instrument. Franklin in a vein of irony made similar comments to those of Henshall and Campbell. He then received a letter from L. L. Pinkerton of Midway, Kentucky—published on February 28, 1860.

> So far as is known to me, or I presume, to you. I am the only 'preacher' in Kentucky in our brotherhood who has publicly advocated the propriety of employing instrumental music in some churches, and that the church of God in Midway is the only church that has yet made a decided effort to introduce it. The calls for your opinion, it is probable, came from those regions.²⁰⁵

It is generally presumed that the instrument was introduced sometime during 1859 and that this is the first time it came to be used permanently. The introduction of the instrument owed its inception to the deplorable singing the congregation did. This singing had degenerated into screeching and brawling that would, as Pinkerton said, 'scare even the rats from worship.' At first it was suggested that a meeting be held on Saturday night to practice the songs. Shortly afterwards, someone brought in a melodeon to be used in getting the right pitch. Before long, one of the sisters was accompanying the singing with her playing on the melodeon. The group observed that the effect of the use of the melodeon was good on the singing, and so it was decided to try to use the instrument on the Lord's Day worship. Thomas Parish played the instrument at worship.²⁰⁶

---

203  *Ibid.*, p. 310.
204  *Ibid.*, p. 310.
205  *Ibid.*, p. 310–11.
206  *Ibid.*, p. 311.

## *Objections*

The presence of the instrument caused considerable friction. The most effective opposition came from Adam Hibler, one of the elders. Late one night Hibler pushed one of his slaves, Reuben, through a window. Reuben passed the melodeon through, and Hibler took it home with him. But another instrument was afterwards brought in and continued in use by the church.[207]

From 1860 onward instruments of music gradually made their way into many churches, and along with the Missionary Society, became an issue of serious debate beginning about 1865.

## Conclusion

Having traced the history of the introduction of the missionary society and instrumental music in worship, it now remains for us to recount the controversy that these two issues raised within a united brotherhood. Division over the Society and instruments was not immediate, but it was inevitable because two distinct viewpoints about "restoration" evolved out of the heated discussions that followed.

The viewpoint of some was that "silence" of the scriptures provides no authority and is therefore prohibitive. Others argued that the "silence" of the scriptures is permissive and allows freedom of choice. We will, in the next chapter, look at these two viewpoints as brethren from 1865 onward tested the meaning and scripturalness of Thomas Campbell's slogan—"Where the scriptures speak, we speak; where the scriptures are silent, we are silent."

## Discussion

1. What did sudden growth in the Restoration Movement create? Who was the principal man who promoted organizations? What did some feel the worship needed? What new and important question did the organizations and instrumental music raise?

2. When did the sudden growth begin? By whose influence? What idea did this growth spur? What did Alexander Campbell expect this growth to produce? What did he oppose in *The Christian Baptist*? What did growth cause him to promote in *The Millennial Harbinger*? When did

---

[207] *Ibid.*, p. 312.

state organizations begin? What year did Campbell call for a national organization?

3. When did the first national organization meet? How many delegates were there? From how many churches? Where did they meet? What, according to Pendleton, was not the purpose of the meeting? Why did they meet? What was this organization called? How often would the society meet? When? Was there any opposition? Who specifically opposed it? What were the specific objections? When did the substantial opposition begin?

4. When was the question of instrumental music first raised? In the response why did Henshall say men needed it? How did Alexander Campbell describe it? What is the second instance on record of an attempt to introduce it? When was it introduced on a permanent basis? By whom? How? Why? How did an elder display his opposition?

5. What developed because of these two innovations? What issue was raised? What did some think about "silence?" What slogan did this controversy test?

# Chapter 11

# A Slogan: Its Test and Meaning

## Introduction

"Where the scriptures speak, we speak; where the scriptures are silent, we are silent" had become the unofficial slogan or motto of the Restoration Movement. Although Thomas Campbell had uttered these words in a sermon in 1808, men of the Restoration Movement in its first 50–60 years had never felt a need to define what he or they meant by it.

By the mid-nineteenth century, however, issues had arisen that challenged the thinking of restoration advocates about the "silence" part of the slogan. Divergent views of the slogan developed to test not only the meaning of the utterance, but to test the strength of the cords of fellowship that bound these advocates together.

In this chapter we will look at two intersections of the silence of the scriptures as relates to missionary societies and instruments in worship. These views and others would ultimately diverge into three different paths and three distinct religious groups … our study in the next chapter.

## The Slogan: Two Views of Silence

A. W. Fortune, in *The Disciples of Kentucky,* succinctly describes the two interpretations of the Restoration Movement:

> There were two different interpretations of the church which inevitably came into conflict. There were those who believed the church should move on with the rest of the world and adapt the spirit of the New Testament to conditions that were ever changing. They held that, when not forbidden by the New Testament, they were free to adapt their program to changing needs. On the other hand, there were those who believed the matter of the church was fixed for all times, and the fact that certain things were not sanctioned was sufficient ground for rejecting them. The men on

both sides were equally honest, but they had a different approach to these issues that were raised.[208]

Lester McAllister and William E. Tucker in *Journey in Faith* relate these two approaches to Thomas Campbell's celebrated slogan and give two views of it. "Many years earlier," they say, "Thomas Campbell unintentionally had laid the foundation for a full-scale debate ... in the *Declaration* and *Address* Campbell proposed that followers of Christ accept the New Testament as the church's constitution. He added: 'Nothing ought to be received into the faith or worship of the church, or be made a term of communion among Christians, that is not as old as the New Testament.' Rejecting all credal affirmations in the interest of restoring 'the ancient order,' Campbell summarized his biblicism in the form of a motto: 'Where the scriptures speak; we speak, where the scriptures are silent, we are silent.'"[209]

In time this expression, accepted as a slogan by Disciples everywhere, created more problems than it solved. Strict constructionists or scholastics among the Disciples insisted that the church's organization and elements of worship must be derived from explicit scripture commands and precedents. 'That which the Bible does not specifically teach is prohibited,' they maintained. The silence of the scriptures was binding to their way of thinking.[210]

On the other hand, progressive disciples were convinced that such legalistic primitivism utterly perverted Thomas Campbell's motto, moderate or progressive disciples retorted that the silence of the New Testament was permissive rather than restrictive. Responding to the strict constructionists, they countered, "That which the Bible does not specifically prohibit is permitted."[211] W. E. Garrison, as Hailey quotes, summarizes the issue by stating that "the crux of it was a difference of opinion as to extent to which the church of today and of all time is limited by the pattern of the primitive church."[212]

W. K. Pendleton, son-in-law of Alexander Campbell and defender of the Missionary Society, speaks the view of the "progressive disciples" and Jacob Creath, who opposed the society speaks the sentiment of the "strict constructionists." Pendleton said:

---

208 Hailey, p. 198.
209 McAlister/Tucker, p. 237.
210 *Ibid.*, p. 237.
211 *Ibid.*, p. 238.
212 Hailey, p. 178.

> Let it not be said, then, that the disciples of Christ are to take the silence of scripture on a given subject as a positive prohibition against all freedom of action or obligation of duty. No rule could be more productive of evil than this.[213]

Creath said:

> You say that our Savior and the apostles did not denounce conventions, as such. Did they denounce popery or corrupt Protestantism, as such? Did they denounce infant baptism, or creed making, or auricular confession, as such? It is for you to show where they *authorized* conventions.[214]

Here we clearly see the battle line drawn for a half-century of debate over missionary societies and instrumental music. Let us now briefly follow the applications of these principles to each issue.

# The Society: Its Defense and Opposition

## *Its Defense*

The society was first proposed and defended by Alexander Campbell. After his death in 1866 the controversy heated up considerably and was defended principally by *The Millennial Harbinger*, *The Christian Standard*, and *The Christian-Evangelist*. In a series of articles on "Church Organization," Campbell wrote:

> "Have we, then, no scriptural model, no divine precedent or authority for any form of church organization and cooperation?" In a later article he answers: "In all things pertaining to public interest, not on Christian faith, piety, or morality, the church of Jesus Christ in its aggregate character, is left free and unshackled by any apostolic authority. This is the great point which I assert as of capital importance in any great conventional movement or cooperation in advancing the public interests of a common Christianity and a common salvation. My strong proof for this conclusion is that, while faith, piety, and morality are all divinely established and enacted by special agents—apostles and prophets possessed of plenary inspiration; matter of prudential arrangement for evangelizing of the world, for the better application of our

---

213  West, p. 54–55.
214  Hailey, p. 203.

means and resources, according to the exigencies of society and the ever-varying complexion of things around us—are left without a single law, statue, ordinance, or enactment in the New Testament.[215]

Note Campbell's emphasis on silence and, in his view, its permissiveness. Campbell clearly saw the society as a matter of expediency.

After Campbell's death, W. K. Pendleton became editor of *The Millennial Harbinger* and one of the chief proponents of the missionary society. Pendleton also argued that the society, based on silence, was a matter of expediency and liberty.

> "You say," he writes, "Your Missionary Society is not scriptural,"—and you mean by this, that there is no special express precept in the Scriptures commanding it. We concede this without a moment's hesitation. There is none; but what do you make of it? Is everything which is not scriptural therefore wrong? Again: Does he say that it is not *positively and expressly commanded;* then we demand by which canon of interpretation does he make mere silence prohibitory? And finally, as noted previously, "Let it not be said, then, that the disciples of Christ are to take the silence of the scriptures on a given subject as a positive rule of the prohibition against all freedom of action or obligation of duty. No rule could be more productive of evil than this.[216]

West comments on the views of Campbell and Pendleton:

> The basic apology for the Society Pendleton based upon his conception of the church universal, and in this he followed closely the reasoning of Alexander Campbell. No man is prepared to see the Society as Pendleton saw it without beginning where Pendleton began. First, he filed his mind with the thought of the church in its universal ("aggregate," Campbell called it; see above, LAS) aspect, ignoring for the time being the local church. God gave the church—in its universal sense—the responsibility to convert the world. But God did not give the method by which the church—in its universal sense—was to convert the world. Therefore, whatever method the church—in its universal sense—uses is acceptable. The method is a matter of expediency. The

---

215  *Ibid.,* p. 203.
216  West, 50–51; 54–55.

church universal is left free to decide for herself. This is briefly the defense he made for it.[217]

Campbell said this regarding expediency: "I do not place meetinghouses, pews, or hymnbooks, on a footing with civil government or the church of God! The building of a meeting house is as conventional as a Bible Society or a missionary society; and he that opposes the one, should, on all premises and logic, opposed the other."[218] Isaac Errett, editor of *The Christian Standard*, took up where Campbell and Pendleton left off and became the chief defender of the society until his death in 1888. James DeForest Murch wrote of Errett:

> In 1866 Isaac Errett began the publication of a new weekly, *The Christian Standard*. Mr. Errett was a strong supporter of the missionary society efforts of the Disciples, and also an advocate of a more liberal interpretation of the old principle of 'speaking where the scriptures speak.' To him is given credit for having saved the principle of church cooperation through societies for the Disciples of Christ.[219]

The defense of societies was clear and basic. Purely and simply, it was a matter of expediency. Yes, they did admit, the Bible is silent on them, but silence is permissive and grants freedom to act according to good common sense. The society, thus, is an effective method or expedient for accomplishing the church universal's mission to preach the gospel to every creature. What, then, did opponents of the society have to say?

## Its Opposition

Jacob Creath, along with two or three churches, were the first to speak out against the missionary society. They were followed by Tolbert Fanning and David Lipscomb in the *Gospel Advocate* and Benjamin Franklin (not the statesman) and John F. Rowe in the *American Christian Review*. Creath argued from the perspective that there was no authority for societies and conventions.

> You say that our Savior and the apostles did not denounce conventions as such. Did they denounce popery or corrupt Protestantism, as such? Did they denounce infant baptism, or creed making, or auricular confession as such? It is for you to show

---
217  *Ibid.*, p. 55.
218  Smith, Vol. 1, p. 198.
219  Christians Only, p. 177.

where they authorized conventions. It will be seen that, in this discussion, the advocates of conventions have totally abandoned the rule on which we and all Protestants set out—that the Bible alone is the religion of Protestants. They have not produced one passage of scripture, to countenance these assemblies from the New Testament.[220]

The Connellsville, Pennsylvania, church responded to the beginning of the society with ten resolutions and additional comments. Under the comments they argued:

> That the church of Jesus Christ, is, in its constitution and design, essentially missionary, we conceive to be an axiomatic truth. Not a missionary society, but emphatically and preeminently *the* missionary society—the only one—authorized by Jesus Christ or sanctioned by the apostles. Her president is Christ; her constitution is the Holy Scriptures and the sanctification of the world. For this purpose, she is fully commission by her great Head, and fully qualified to fulfill that commission. To affirm that she is not competent, is to charge her all-wise Founder with the inconsistency of assigning her a duty which she is unable to perform. If then, she is authorized and competent, all other societies for this purpose are not only unscriptural, but they are unnecessary and uncalled for. Unscriptural, because they appropriate to themselves the duty and honor which rightfully belong to the church; unnecessary, because the end for which they are instituted the church is fully able to accomplish.[221]

The Connellsville letter also argued its premise that the missionary society is a separate organization from the church and not merely a method.

> We know it is thought by some, that these societies are not separate and apart from the church, but part and parcel of her. But by a little reflection, it will be seen, that although they may not be entirely composed of members of the church, (which is not often the case), yet they are separate and distinct from her, as much so as any Free Mason or Temperance Society composed of church members. Her president is not the president of any of them; her constitution is not the constitution of any of them; her laws are not their laws; she has an initiatory rite—they have initiatory fees;

---

220  *Ibid.*, p. 203.
221  Hailey, p. 167.

and but comparatively few of her members are members of any or all of them. Hence, it followed that they are distinct organizations, separate and apart from the church.[222]

In 1855 Tolbert Fanning started *The Gospel Advocate*, in his own words "to give the subject of cooperation a thorough examination."[223] Fanning emphasized the views that the church is the only divinely authorized organization for converting the world and that it is a fully competent to accomplish this task. He also emphasized, as Creath and others, the absence of authority for missionary societies. David Lipscomb became coeditor of the *Advocate* in 1866 and maintained the views of Creath and Fanning.

In 1856 Benjamin Franklin began publishing the *American Christian Review* in which he at first vacillated between favoring and opposing the missionary society. By 1866 Franklin had settled his mind and became the fiercest opponent of all human organizations. John F. Rowe became assistant editor of the *Review* in 1878 and joined Franklin in opposing the societies. Their arguments differ little from those already presented.

The chief argument against the society was their lack of scriptural authority. But how much was made of the sufficiency of local congregations, as in the first century, to accomplish the work of evangelism? Human organization were mere substitutes for the divine body and cast a reflection on the wisdom and plan of God. In both defense and criticism of the missionary society, there is a clear difference of views regarding the silence of the scriptures. To its defenders, "silence" is permissive and to its opponents, "silence" is prohibitive.

# Instrumental Music: Its Defense and Opposition

## *Its Defense*

Moses Lard, editor of *The Lord's Quarterly*, succinctly summarized and stated the issue: "The question of instrumental music in the churches of Christ involves a great sacred principle … that principle is the right of men to introduce innovations into the prescribed worship of God. This right we utterly deny. The advocates of instrumental music affirm it. This makes the issue."[224]

---

222  *Ibid.*, p. 168.
223  West, Vol. 1, p. 205–07.
224  Hailey, p. 215.

J. W. McGarvey, whom many view as the greatest scholar of the Restoration Movement, "pled that brethren would lay aside all feelings pro and con, and start anew with the inquiry: 'Ought we make use of musical instruments in public worship?' He asked the brethren to come out with their views on it, concluding, 'Let us, then, have the question discussed and finally settled.'" McGarvey saw the defense of musical instruments in worship as either *scriptural* or *expedient*. He called for a discussion of both. "If instrumental music were in the Bible, and if God by his written word approved it then, let us have the scriptures, McGarvey would say. If it is not in the Bible, McGarvey pled that the whole ground of expediency be given a thorough examination."[225]

The first to discuss the issue were McGarvey and A. S. Hayden in 1865. McGarvey opened the discussion by "examining the scriptures so commonly used by those declaring the word of God favored it." An example is seen in McGarvey's response to its use by the Jews as a basis for use in the church. West summarizes:

> McGarvey, as well as many other pioneers, saw that the very fact that the church, when established, rejected the use of the Jewish worship of the Old Testament, was proof enough that the instrument was not suited to the worship in the church. The worship of the Jews was particularly fitted for the economy under which they lived. Their worship consisted of offering sacrifices, ceremonial washings, burning incense, and the use of instruments of music, among other things. The church on the other hand is the realization of an entirely different economy, fully scriptural in scope. Here God chose a worship where the worshipper, directly from his heart worshipped the Lord without the aid of incense, animal sacrifice, or mechanical instruments. McGarvey then, ... closed by saying, 'Now, Brother Hayden, if this argument is valid, I would again repeat that every man who bows to the authority of God's word, must oppose the use of instrumental music in the church.[226]

Hayden made it clear that he was not advocating the use of the instrument, which meant, as such statements have always meant, that with him it was on the plain of expediency. He replied only because he thought he saw weaknesses in McGarvey's argument, Hayden maintaining that the silence of the scriptures was not sufficient ground for rejecting it. Although efforts were made to justify by scripture mechanical instruments of music in

225 West, Vol. 1, p. 314.
226 West, p. 315.

worship, they were by and large advocated, as with Hayden, by "silence" and "expediency."[227]

McGarvey took the opposite view on "silence."

> We cannot, therefore, by any possibility, know that a certain element of worship is acceptable to God in the Christian dispensation, when the scriptures which speak of that dispensation are silent in reference to it. To introduce any such element is unscriptural and presumptuous. It is will worship, if any such thing as will worship can exist. On this ground we condemn the burning of incenses, the lighting of candles, the wearing of priestly robes, and the reading of printed prayers. On the same ground we condemn instrumental music.[228]

Isaac Errett, who became editor of *The Christian Standard* in 1866, and Benjamin Franklin, editor of *The American Christian Review*, took up the debate in their respective papers—Errett justifying it and Franklin opposing it.

Speaking of Franklin and his periodical, *The Review*, Errett said, "The *Review* regards the use of instruments as an attempt to introduce a new element of worship and exclaims against it as utterly wanting in divine authority. The *Standard* regards it as an expedient, proposed to aid the church to perform, in an edifying way, the duty of singing … The *Review* admits expedients—means of obeying the divine precept to sing—such as hymnbooks, notebooks, tuning forks, etc., …Why then, raise such a clamor about instruments? Why may they not be treated as expedients, and a decision reached for or against them as such?"[229]

Franklin's view was that to be acceptable it must be "written" or "prescribed" in revelation. "We can remain on safe ground, the common ground, and the ground on which we have stood in peace and war—on what is *written*. The worship in all its parts—all its elements—is a matter of *revelation, divinely prescribed*. Nothing is acceptable worship, only that which the Lord ordained."[230]

Robert Richardson, co-laborer with Alexander Campbell in *The Millennial Harbinger*, and at Bethany College and Campbell's biographer, made a significant and telling point about expediency. Said Richardson:

---

227 *Ibid.*, p. 314.
228 Hailey, p. 207.
229 *Ibid.*, p. 219.
230 West, Vol. 2, p. 86.

As regards the use of musical instruments in church worship, the case is wholly different. This can never be a question of expediency, for the simple reason that there is no law prescribing or authorizing it. If it were anywhere said in the New Testament that Christians should use instruments, then it would become a question of expediency what kind of instrument was to be used, whether an organ or a melodeon, the "loud-sounding cymbals' or the 'light guitar'; whether it should cost $50, or $500, or $1000; and what circumstances should regulate the performance. It happens, however, that this is nowhere said; and, consequently, no such questions of expediency can ever arise in a church that is truly and really governed by the law of the Lord.

> For the proper question is not, 'Is it expedient? Nor does it assist the singing? Nor is it not as lawful to use a musical instrument in the church as in a social circle? ... but is there any law for it? Have we a 'thus saith the Lord' for it? Have we an approved precedent for it among the primitive churches? Nay: it is perfectly well known that there is not a shadow of authority in the Christian scriptures for it, and that instrumental music was not practiced by the primitive Christians. [231]

Richardson then commends the proper approach in discussing this issue:

> A writer in the *Standard*, indeed, attempted some time ago to show that musical instruments were actually commanded, because it is implied in the word 'psalms.' This effort was altogether in the right direction and afforded quite a contrast to the far-fetched sophistries of others who sought to justify the use of instruments by something else than the law of Christ.

Later, Richardson refers to his response to this argument:

> I think I showed, in noticing the argument based upon the word *psalms* that the law authorizing the exercise of singing not only does not imply the use of musical instruments, but in its very terms prohibits this, as incapable of fulfilling any of the requirements of the law. I have seen no attempt to set aside these arguments. [232]

While a few brethren sought to justify musical instruments in worship by scriptural authority, the issue mainly settled on the question of expediency

---

231  Hailey, p. 216.
232  *Ibid.*, p. 217.

and the silence of the scripture. Silence to its defends meant the freedom to use it and to its opponents a lack of authority to introduce it. J. S. Lamar, who felt the instrument was not inconsistent with New Testament teaching, wrote in *The Millennial Harbinger*: "I must contend, therefore, that 'within the word is authority—all beyond is liberty.' This statement may be expanded to read: 'What the scriptures declare or necessarily imply, is law; anything not inconsistent with law, belongs to the domain of freedom.'"[233]

Moses E. Lard, who viewed the instrument as an innovation, wrote in his *Quarterly*: Every man among us must stand nobly up for the following position: *In all acts of worship, we must do only what is prescribed in the New Testament, or was done with divine sanction by the primitive Christians.* Not the semblance of innovation must be allowed or this sacred principle.[234]

## Conclusion

It is only fair to point out that some men, such as McGarvey, Lard, F. G. Allen, etc., on the basis of "silence" justified the society and condemned musical instruments. West notes:

> McGarvey, I. E. Grubbs, Allen, lard, and S. A. Kelley each believed in organized societies and defended them vigorously upon the ground of expediency. They were, on the other hand, bitter enemies of the instrument in worship. Men of their mind in middle Kentucky were slow to agree that both the society and the instrument stood on the same principle. As the fact slowly dawned on many, the 'middle ground' faded away.[235]

What is apparent in the debate over societies and musical instruments is that the two opposing sides cannot long live together in harmonious fellowship. The divergent interpretations of Campbell's slogan must gradually lead the two sides into different and opposite directions, as the later history of the two verifies.

Division did not occur officially between the Churches of Christ and Christian Churches until the twentieth century, but some called for separation long before it was reflected in the religious census of 1906. While the Churches of Christ and Christian Churches were parting ways a division was already at work among Christian Churches that would soon lead to

---

233  *Ibid.*, p. 220.
234  *Ibid.*, p. 214.
235  West, Vol. 2, p. 183.

Independent Christian Churches and Disciples of Christ—a three way split that will be detailed in the next chapter.

## Discussion

1. What slogan became the unofficial motto of the Restoration Movement? How long before men began to define it? What part of the motto came under debate? What specific issues arose to test the meaning of the slogan?

2. What was the view of the "strict constructionists?" Of the "progressives?" What is the crux of the issue? What did Pendleton oppose? What did Creath demand?

3. What did Campbell-Pendleton see as grounds for the society? How did they argue for the universal church? Campbell paralleled the society to what other matters? Who defended societies in the *The Christian Standard*? Who was the chief opponent of the society? What did Connellsville say was God's missionary society? Who opposed the society in *The Gospel Advocate*? Name two. Who in the *American Christian Review*? Name two.

4. What made the issue? What did McGarvey call for? What two approaches were possible to justify it? Who opposed McGarvey in the beginning of the debate? What paper was for it? Who was its editor? What paper opposed it? Who was its editor? What did Richardson say about expediency? How did Lamar argue for it? How did Lard argue against it?

5. What is the middle-of-the-road view? Who held it? What would the divergent views ultimately produce? When did the division come officially? How many groups grew out of the divison?

Chapter 12

# Division: Three Separate Groups

## Introduction

The Restoration Movement, an effort to bring unity to the religious world, found itself on the brink of division following the introduction of the American Christian Missionary Society and the practice of worshiping with instruments of music. Other serious issues arose by the end of the nineteenth century and the division that was inevitable between Churches of Christ and Christian Churches threatened to divide Christian Churches further and produce a three-way split.

When all the issues had been debated and the furor had settled, the Restoration Movement had produced three distinct religious bodies: Churches of Christ; Independent Christian Churches; Disciples of Christ. In this chapter we will take a brief look at the issues, the principal influences, and the settled state of each of these groups.

## Division: Churches of Christ and Christian Churches

From 1865 to 1906 there was a proliferation of societies of all kinds and instruments being introduced into the worship. These, specifically the instrument, were the main cause of the first division. The introduction of new organizations in addition to the American Christian Missionary Society began in 1874 with the Christian Woman's Board of Missions. Then followed the Foreign Christian Missionary Society (1875), National Benevolent Association (1886), Board of Church Extension (1888), Board of Education (1894), Board of Ministerial Relief (1895). These would later be organized under the control of the United Christian Missionary Society in 1920.[236]

Even though during the war, the instrument was fought severely as an innovation, its use at first grew slowly and then more rapidly. Ben Franklin declared in 1867 that not ten congregations in the brotherhood were using the instrument, but by 1885 that number had greatly multiplied.[237] By

---
236 Garrison/DeGroot, p. 521.
237 West, Vol. 2, p. 226.

the 1870s a steady flow of churches began to introduce instruments into worship. Frankfort, Kentucky (1872); Augusta, Georgia (1875/76); Bowling Green, Kentucky (1879); East Cleveland, Ohio (1881); Anderson, Indiana (1882); Wellington, Kansas (1884).[238]

Where the instrument was introduced caused brethren to be faced with two basic choices. Stay and compromise their convictions or leave and start a new work. J. M. Mathis, one of Indiana's pioneer preachers, had always opposed the use of the instrument just as he had the missionary society. When the society was accepted by most of the brethren in 1849, he surrendered his opposition in deference to their wishes. His last years were spent near Bedford, IN. He watched Indiana churches adding the instrument. He never relinquished his opposition and yet wrote: 'I am opposed to the organ in worship but make no factious opposition to it. I suffer no organ to drive me from my place in the church of Christ, nor from my duty as a disciple of Christ.'[239] J. W. McGarvey wrote, "I have not withdrawn my opposition to the organ. I would not hold membership with, nor contract to preach for a church using one. Its introduction against the conscientious protest of a minority is high handed wickedness and can be prompted by no spirit but that of the world and the flesh.[240] After 50 years of preaching McGarvey was forced in 1902 to leave the Broadway church in Lexington when the instrument was introduced."[241]

As the instrument began to be introduced many brethren, as McGarvey, took their leave and started new congregations. West mentions several examples among which is this account:

> Late in 1880 the church in Bedford, Indiana, put in the instrument. Uncle "Stever" Younger, who had given one thousand dollars on a new building, had worked hard in building up the congregation. When the organ was interjected into the worship, he and fifty others were excluded. A short time earlier the church in Bloomington, Indiana, had a similar experience. W. B. F. Treat came to Bloomington in 1870 and preached for the church four years. Afterward he turned his attention to evangelistic work, although still making Bloomington his home. Weak preaching produced weak members in the years that followed. The sermons were more lectures or moralizing, 'such as would be popular in any sectarian church.'

---

238  *Ibid.*, p. 226.229.
239  *Ibid.*, p. 230.
240  *Ibid*, p. 233.
241  See West, p. 442.

The organ was introduced. Treat and some others left and began meeting in the courthouse. The introduction of the organ took place in November 1877.[242]

By about 1880 brethren began to speak of a possible division within the ranks of the Restoration Movement because of innovations. West in his writing recounts the statements of three leading men:

W. B. F. Treat said, in 1879,

> The last few years have been eventful ones in our history and by experience we have received lessons which some of us had hoped to never learn. It is strictly true that we can never divide while, as individuals and as congregations, we have the grand watchword with which this movement began: 'Where the Bible speaks, we speak; where the Bible is silent, we are silent …' If the worldly, unauthorized customs and practices that are popular with the innovationists and sectarians are forced into the church, over the protests of godly men, division is not only imminent, but it may become a necessity and a virtue! The law of Christian unity is based upon the recognition of the supreme authority of Christ; and nothing in the gospel of Christ requires a believer to submit to unauthorized practice in religion.[243]

John F. Rowe, who succeeded Benjamin Franklin as editor of *The American Christian Review* in 1878, said in an 1883 editorial:

> If, however, in their struggles at the post of duty and as faithful members in one body, the true Israel of God are overpowered and the church of Christ loses its apostolic identity by the presence of organized ecclesiasticism and priestly domination, in that it will become necessary, according to the mandates of God quoted above, to actually separate and make a new rally upon the original ground.[244]

In 1885 McGarvey said:

> I have but little sympathy with those brethren who seem to dread disunion among ourselves as the direst of all evils. If we would inspire sensible men around us with a desire for union with us, we must be careful to show them that we do not and will not maintain

---

242  *Ibid.*, p. 227.
243  *Ibid.*, p. 222–24.
244  *Ibid.*, p. 222–24.

unity with anything unscriptural, whether it shows itself within our ranks or outside them. Truth first, union afterwards, and union only in truth. This is our motto.[245]

## *Who's to Blame*

The question of who is to blame for the division came up for considerable discussion as the division began to take place in congregation after congregation. Each, as one would expect, blamed the other.

Isaac Errett, editor of *The Christian Standard* and the chief spokesman for the Christian Churches, said as early as 1872:

> The greatest danger that we see is that of making tests of fellowship of opinions or expedients concerning which we have no right to judge one another. Let us be careful at this point and we are safe.[246]

In 1883 Errett wrote again:

> It is becoming growingly evident that the way is thus prepared for an attempted division in our ranks ... Let our brethren be on their guard against every attempt, secret or open, to create division among us. There is nothing to justify it. It can only be done by the introduction of false tests of fellowship.[247]

By "false tests of fellowship," Errett referred to opposition to societies and instruments of music by those he called "factionists." Assuming however, that these are mere expedients begs the question. It demands biblical proof.

Writing in the *Gospel Advocate*, James A. Harding in 1884 noted:

> There are many whom we are told to 'mark' and 'avoid;' men from whom we are to 'withdraw' ourselves; men who trouble the churches of God by forcing upon them untaught questions; who gratify their own tastes by forcing organs and other things into the worship, thereby driving numbers of the oldest and best members out. From such let us turn away. It is worthy to remark that the things that are troubling the churches are the inventions of men; the organ, the human missionary society, the suppers, and festivals for raising money, etc., are the bones of contention ... Did not the apostles get along without organs? Yes! Are not these divisive? Yes! They have rent more churches, alienated more brethren, and caused

---

245  *Ibid.*, p. 224.
246  *Ibid.*, p. 224.
247  *Ibid.*, p. 248.

more heartaches among the children of God than any other things that have troubled the Zion of our King in this century.[248]

The issue of blame rests on the scripturalness of the societies and musical instruments in worship. If they are unscriptural, then those who introduced them are at fault for the division. If, on the other hand, they are mere expedients to carry out a law of God, then those who oppose them are at fault.

## **Division Comes**

Division was inevitable and already prevalent in many places by the end of the 1880s. It was then the first call for a clear-cut division was issued. It is usually referred to as the *Sand Creek Address and Declaration*.

> On Sunday, August 18, 1889, six thousand members of the church gathered in Shelby County, IL, at the site of the old Sand Creek congregation in a great mass-meeting. Since 1873 large masses of brethren had congregated at this site to enjoy a few days of fellowship; and to have opportunities of hearing prominent preachers. On this particular Sunday in 1889 the taciturn audience listened for an hour and forty minutes while Daniel Somer spoke on the condition of the church. Somer charged the 'innovators' with being responsible for all the division, discord, bitterness, and strife within the church. He proclaimed that they had constantly asked these men not to push their innovations, but they had been refused. The missionary society and instrumental music were being pushed into the churches, driving a wedge between brethren. What then, was to be done?[249]

A few excerpts from the *Address* highlight the reasons for division and what several brethren thought should be done:

> Brethren, you doubtless know that we, as disciples of Christ with scarcely an exception, many long years ago took the position that in matters of doctrine and practice, religious, 'Where the Bible speaks, we speak, and where the Bible is silent, we are silent.' Further, we held that nothing should be taught, received, or practiced, religiously, for which we could not produce a 'Thus saith the Lord.' And, doubtless, many of you also know that as long as the above principles were clearly and faithfully observed, we were a prosperous

---

248  *Ibid.*, p. 239.
249  *Ibid.*, p. 431.

and happy people. Then we were of one heart and one soul; we lived in peace and prospered in the things pertaining to the kingdom of God and the name of our Lord Jesus Christ.

It is perhaps needless for us to add, in this connection, that we as a people, discarded all man-made laws, rules, disciplines, and confessions of faith as means of governing the church. We have always acknowledged, and do now acknowledge, the all-sufficiency of the Holy Scriptures to govern us as individuals and as congregations.

There are those among us who do teach, and practice things not taught or found in the New Testament, which have been received by many well-meaning disciples, but rejected by those more thoughtful, and in most instances better informed in the scriptures, and who have repeatedly protested this false teaching and those corrupt practices among the disciples. Some of the things of which we hereby complain, and against which we protest, are the unlawful methods resorted to in order to raise or get money for religious purposes, viz., that of the church holding festivals of various kinds, in the house of the Lord, or elsewhere, demanding that each participant shall pay a certain sum as an admittance fee; the use of instrumental music in the worship; the select choir, to the virtual, if not the real, abandonment of congregational singing. Likewise, the man-made society for missionary work and the one-man, imported preacher pastor to feed and watch over the flock. These, with many other objectionable and unauthorized things, are now taught and practiced in many of the congregations, and that to the great grief and mortification of some of the members of said congregations.

And now we say that we beg of you that you turn away speedily at once from such things, and remember that though we are the Lord's freedmen, yet we are bound by the authority of our Lord Jesus Christ … Therefore, brethren, without addressing you further by using other arguments, and without going further in detailing these unpleasant, as we see them, vicious things, you must allow us. … to declare that we cannot tolerate the things of which we complain, for if we do, we are (in a measure, at least) blamable ourselves.

And now, in closing up this address and declaration, we state that we are impelled from a sense of duty to say that all such as are guilty of teaching or allowing and practicing the many innovations and corruptions to which we have referred, after having had sufficient time for mediation and reflection, if they will not turn away from such abominations, that we cannot and will not regard them as brethren.[250]

The date for the division is listed as 1906 because this is the year that the first religious census lists "Churches of Christ" and "Christian Churches" separately. West comments:

> And so, by 1906, the work of division had taken its full course. The 'Christian Churches' or 'Disciples of Christ,' as they preferred to be called, took their instruments and their missionary society, and walked a new course. The battle had been long, treacherous, costly, and bitter. Many brethren, still licking their wounds, looked to the future to start all over again.[251]

# Division: Independent Christian Churches and Disciples of Christ

The second division cannot be understood apart from the history of "liberal theology," or "modernism" that infiltrated the Disciples of Christ. So say McAllister and Tucker:

> The storm of protest—which eventually gave birth to another restoration body known as 'Christian Churches and Churches of Christ' (instrumental, LAS)—cannot be understood without taking into full account the impact of American liberal theology around the turn of the century and thereafter.[252]

This theology denied verbal inspiration of the Bible, the deity of Christ, the transcendence of God, and the creation of man as the following quote emphasizes:

> The genius of liberal theology was its openness to all truth and its insistence on genuine dialogue between church and world. Fearing nothing more than an outmoded faith, liberals reconstructed Christian theology to harmonize it with prevailing currents in philosophy and science. Their emphasis on historical optimism, the immanence of God, the dignity of man, and the humanity

---

250  *Ibid.*, p. 431–32.
251  *Ibid.*, p. 448.
252  McAllister/Tucker, p. 361.

of Christ stood in vivid contrast to traditional Christianity. Exponents of liberalism resolved the apparent conflict between Moses and Darwin by insisting that evolution could have been God's way of doing things. They defended the principles of biblical criticism on the ground that the Bible was not only the record of divine revelation but also an intensely human connection of documents.[253]

American liberal theology seeped into the Disciples of Christ by way of Yale, Union in New York, and the University of Chicago. These influences changed the educational approach of the Disciples. "Advances in ministerial education among Disciples played a major role in shaping the battle over the Bible. Prior to the 1890s educated Disciples preachers with few exceptions had prepared for the ministry in little denominational colleges which awarded no degree beyond a Bachelor of Arts. Thereafter divinity students in increasing numbers found their way to the nations great theological center."[254]

L.L. Pinkerton as early as the 1860s had questioned the inspiration of the Bible and Isaac Errett had rejected the infallibility of the scriptures as early as 1883, but R. C. Cave was the first manifestation of those who had totally surrendered to "liberal theology." The revolt against the traditional formulation of the Christian faith did not inflame Disciples until the winter of 1889–90. At the time Robert C. Cave (1843–1923), outspoken minister of the Central Christian Church in St. Louis, preached a series of sermons which shocked the congregation. From the pulpit of the church, he argued that God did not command Abraham to slay his son or require Jephthah to offer his daughter in sacrifice. In interpreting the New Testament message, he advocated 'open membership error,' denied the virgin birth and the bodily resurrection of Jesus and asserted that Christians might believe Christ to be a myth so long as they accepted 'the Christ idea.'[255]

J. W. McGarvey, writing in Biblical criticism in *The Christian Standard,* took issue with the modernists and wrote a column from 1893–1911 opposing their liberal views. Murch speaks strongly about McGarvey's influence: "But it was McGarvey," he writes, "above all others in the brotherhood, who sensed the real issues at stake in both the Great Apostasy and the

---

253  Ibid., p. 362.
254  Ibid., p. 371.
255  Ibid., p. 364.

Great Controversy and dealt effectively with them. Without in him the conservatives would have been dispersed and overcome."[256]

J. W. McGarvey served as a field general for the Cincinnati paper (*Standard*, LAS) in its war on the critics. His conception of the Bible was typical of the conservative mind. Since the Bible is the Word of God, it must be verbally inspired and absolutely inerrant. According to the infallible scriptures, Moses wrote the Pentateuch and David the Psalms; Jonah spent three days in the belly of a whale, and God literally created woman from Adam's rib. Describing McGarvey's point of view, one commentator wrote: 'Isaiah was Isaiah, Daniel was Daniel, Job was Job, Jonah in particular was Jonah, the great fish and all, and Balaam's ass spoke as good Hebrew as his master, and what else?' To say less, in McGarvey's opinion, impugned the veracity of the scriptures. He consequently did everything in his power to protect the bible from the plunder of 'destructive critics.'[257] McGarvey's chief combatant was H. L. Willett, "a colleague of Dr. Harper in the department of Semitics at Chicago and dean of the Disciples Divinity House"—McGarvey writing in *The Christian Standard* and Willett writing in the *Christian Evangelist*.[258]

Liberalism was introduced to the mainstream of the Restoration Movement by the Disciples Divinity House, *The Christian Century,* The Campbell Institute, and the Congresses promoted by a small coterie of 'forward looking brethren.'[259] These were the media by which the propaganda of modernism gained a foothold in the Christian Churches and secured control of most major organizations, agencies, and institutions.

At the 1893 national convention, convened in Chicago, President Harper urged Disciples to undertake such an enterprise. The following May it was announced that the Disciples Divinity House of the University of Chicago had been constituted and that Herbert L. Willett had been selected dean of the institution. "Of its beginning and influence," McAllister and Tucker say, "Despite heavy opposition, Disciples Divinity House opened in the fall of 1884 and survived to become for several decades a dominant factor in Disciples life and thought. The signal success of the enterprise was due in large measure to the leadership of three individuals who served successively as dean of the house: Herbert L. Willett, Winfred E. Garrison, and Edward Scribner Ames. Joined by Charles Morrison Clayton, long-term editor

---

256 Murch, p. 241.
257 McAllister/Tucker, p. 368.
258 Garrison/DeGroot, p. 419.
259 Murch, p. 237–38.

of the *Christian Century* in Chicago, these men literally constituted the intellectual center of the Disciples for many years. Brilliant and determined, they led the Stone-Campbell movement into and through the heyday of liberal theology. "Through their teaching and writing, and that of their students," wrote Ronald E. Osborn, "they brought home to Disciples, too long isolated from the currents of contemporary thinking, the full impact of liberalism."[260]

Willett, Garrison, and Ames were instrumental in forming the Campbell Institute during the 1896 national convention of Disciples at Springfield, Illinois. The organization restricted its membership to college graduates and adopted a threefold purpose.[261]

- To encourage a scholarly spirit.
- To inspire contributions to literature and thought of Disciples.
- To promote spiritual maturity.

The institute became the medium for the development of a liberal strategy for the capture of the schools and agencies of the Disciples. Some have argued that "as a liberalizing force," this small organization's influence was out of proportion to its size.[262]

The principal means by which the scholarship of the larger Christian community filtered into the thought and life of the churches was the congress of the Disciples of Christ.[263] "Liberals," Murch says, "got their idea from the Parliament of Religions held in connection with the World's Fair in Chicago in 1893. Here Christian ministers and scholars mingled with the Jews, Buddhists, Mohammadeans, Shintoists, Confucionists, and persons of heathen faiths ... following one of the interdenominational meetings at Macatawa Park, on Lake Michigan, a group of liberal Disciples laid plans for a serios of Congresses where religious, theological, scientific, and social problems could be discussed at length. The first one was held in St. Louis in 1899 ... in 1912 at Kansas City, a constitution was adopted which widened the orbit of the Congresses to include 'the Baptists and other denominations.' Liberal domination of these meetings and their purpose to use them for liberal propaganda was blatantly demonstrated in the program for 1914."[264]

---

260  McAllister/Tucker, p. 373–74.
261  *Ibid.*, p. 374.
262  *Ibid.*, p. 375.
263  Garrison/DeGroot, p. 444.
264  Murch, p. 240–41.

The *Christian Oracle*, founded in 1884, barely managed to survive. Moved from Des Moines to Chicago in 1888 and renamed the *Christian Century* in 1900, it was offered for sale eight years later. Charles Clayton Morrison (1874–1966), pastor of the Monroe St. Christian Church in Chicago, paid the purchase price of $1500 and launched his career in religious journalism. Under his vigorous leadership the *Christian Century* gradually cut its denominational ties and in 1918 became a "undenominational journal of religion."[265] Of the paper, Garrison and DeGroot say, "A new era of frank commitment to liberalism, but still within the ranks of the Disciples, began in 1980, when Charles Clayton Morrison bought the paper."[266] By 1911, Morrison was promoting open membership among the Disciples—a subject we will say more about momentarily.

## Unbearable Issues

When liberal theology or modernism by these avenues had spread its contagion throughout the Christian Churches, certain viewpoints and practices became unbearable to a small contingent and division once again became inevitable.

### Open Membership

Open membership refers to the view of many that members of other churches ought to be received on faith regardless of whether they have been immersed. "Dr. L. L. Pinkerton in 1869 emerged as the first true 'liberal,' among the reformers, arguing not only for the admission of the unimmersed but also against the prevailing doctrine of the inerrancy of the Bible." The churches were hardly ready for it that early on. "Thomas Munnell, an elder statesman, whose former articles showed the liberal bent of his mind, and who had been secretary of the American Christian Missionary Society in the 1860s, came out in the April, 1894, issue, *New Christian Quarterly*, in favor of waiving the requirement of immersion in the interest of union, treating it as the Apostle Paul did circumcision and as the early church did Jewish sacrifice" But "the actual practice of welcoming the unimmersed into church membership did not begin before 1900."[267]

On December 5, 1906, the Monroe St. Church, Chicago, C.C. Morrison, pastor, became the first congregation of Disciples to accept the "London Plan," for which W. T. Moore had long contended. This meant continuing

---

265  McAllister/Tucker, p. 328.
266  Garrison/DeGroot, p. 431.
267  McAllister/Tucker, p. 390–91, 393.

to practice immersion for all not previously baptized, but accepting into full membership those candidates who were satisfied with their previous baptismal experience ... in May 1919, an official resolution if persons from other churches and those coming from a confession of faith might be received as members of the church with or without baptism, according to their personal conviction.[268]

The *Standard* called another pre-convention rally at Cincinnati in 1919 of "all who are resolved to maintain the Restoration plea intact." This "Restoration Congress" adopted a resolution saying, "Since certain among us are advocating and practicing "open membership," this Congress would express the conviction that such persons and churches have apostatized from the Restoration Movement and should be so regarded by the agencies that serve us."[269]

## Denominational Federation

Many Disciples sought to federate with other denominations who by 1906 were organizing the Federal Council of Churches to share in the common causes such as solving society's social problems. At the 1902 national convention of Disciples in Omaha, Nebraska—"A resolution approving the federation principle was introduced by J.H. Garrison, editor of the *Christian Evangelist*. J. A. Lord, editor of *The Christian Standard,* raised a question whether such an action would not be 'recognizing the denominations' ... the resolution was adopted, with only a small audible opposing voice." At a mass meeting in Norfolk, Virginia, in 1907 approval, with only the objection of J. B. Briney, was given to "the appointment of delegates to the Federal Council."[270] This, added to the practice of open membership, widened the breach between the two contending parties of "liberals," and "conservatives."

## The United Christian Missionary Society

The UCMS was created by the Cincinnati convention of 1919. It embraced the following agencies:[271]

- Foreign Christian Missionary Society
- American Christian Missionary Society
- National Benevolent Association
- Christian Women's Board of Missions
- Board of Ministerial Relief
- Board of Church Extension

---

268 Garrison/DeGroot, p. 434.
269 *Ibid.*, p. 435.
270 *Ibid.*, p. 409.
271 *Ibid.*, p. 428–29.

On this Murch writes:

> In 1919 plans were announced for a merger of all the brotherhood agencies, including the foreign society, into one huge ecclesiastical body. This was done in the name of greater efficiency, the elimination of overlapping organization, and 'constant and conflicting' appeals to the churches for money.' Again, *Christian Standard* sensed the liberal strategy as to move to control not only the Foreign Society, but all the organized life of the brotherhood, as an apparatus to accomplish the liberals' ultimate purposes.[272]

A preconvention rally of conservatives failed to stop the move and the United Christian Missionary Society became a reality that year.

These principal issues, along with the growth of modernistic theology, continued to fester among conservatives and liberals until 1927 when the conservatives formed the North American Christian Convention. After 1927, as McAllister and Tucker note, "Conservatives continued to designate themselves as members of the Disciples of Christ, but in reality, they constituted an identifiable group moving inexorably toward a separate fellowship. After 1955, following a lengthy period of study and discussion, Disciples began the complex process of reorganizing the Christian Church (Disciples of Christ). Consequently, over 3000 congregations with an estimated membership exceeding 750,000 took legal action to withdraw from the fellowship. Then in 1971 the *Yearbook of American Churches* was asked to list the "Christian Churches" and "Churches of Christ (instrumental, LAS) as a separate religious communion."[273]

## Conclusion

According to Garrison and DeGroot the Disciples numbered 1, 905,835 in 1955 and, of that total, according to McAllister and Tucker, the Independent Christian Churches consisted of more than 750,000.[274] In 1960, Murch says, speaking of Churches of Christ, "authentic statistical sources listed 16,500 churches located in every state in the union with a membership of 2, 025,000."[275]

If these statistics be correct, it shows clearly that the missionary society was not a "more efficient" means of evangelizing the world. All it really

---

272  Murch, p. 246.
273  McAllister/Tucker, p. 383–86.
274  Garrison/DeGroot, p. 410; McAllister/Tucker, p. 386.
275  Murch, p. 309.

accomplished, along with other issues, of course, was to divide a united brotherhood into three separate groups.

Despite the failure or inefficiency of extra organizational structures supported by the church, similar issues arose among Churches of Christ after 1906, dividing once more a united brotherhood. We will look at some of that history in the final chapter.

## Discussion

1. What put the Restoration Movement on the brink of division? How many ways did the movement divide? What were the names of the divided groups?

2. What grew in number between 1865 and 1906? What societies were established? Where were instruments introduced? What choices did opposing brethren have? What did brethren generally do when the instrument was introduced? Who was to blame for the division? What address and declaration called for division? When was the division officially recognized?

3. What must be understood to understand this division? What were some of the views of "liberal theology?" What universities promoted these views? Who were the earliest men to show liberal tendencies? Who was the first full liberal theologian to speak up? Who was the principal opponent of liberal theology? List four avenues of liberal theology. What three unbearable issues precipitated the division? What three dates mark the various stages of division?

4. What statistically was the size of the three groups in 1955? What do these statistics say about the need of missionary societies to grow and musical instruments to keep up with the denominations?

# Chapter 13

# Churches of Christ: A History of New Controversies

## Introduction

Following the controversy over missionary societies and musical instruments in worship, by 1906 those in the Churches of Christ saw that unity and fellowship with Christian Churches was impossible. A separate census was taken in 1906 and from then onward the Churches of Christ became a distinct religious movement of independent, autonomous congregations. As a survey from 1906 to the present will show, the Churches of Christ have not been totally free of controversy and divisive issues.

The present controversies, as the ones over the missionary societies and musical instruments, arose over the meaning and truthfulness of Thomas Campbell's slogan—"Where the scriptures speak, we speak; where the scriptures are silent, we are silent."

## Chronology: A Survey of Events, Institutions, and Dates

### *Colleges*

The rise of "Christian" colleges as adjuncts of the home in which young people can study the Bible while they train themselves for secular pursuits is an important factor in the controversy that developed by mid-century. All the colleges operate under boards as separate organizations from any local church.

#### Freed-Hardeman

Beginning as early as 1885 and continuing under several different names, this school received the name "Freed-Hardeman College" in 1919, to pay respect to its two leaders, A. G. Freed and N. B. Hardeman.

#### David Lipscomb

Known at its inception in 1891 as "Nashville Bible School," it was renamed "David Lipscomb College" after the death of Lipscomb in 1917—and honor bestowed on its principal founder.

## Abilene

From its start in 1906, "Abilene Christian College" has maintained the same name (now University)—after the Texas city where it is located.

## Harding

An amalgamation of several small colleges that began earlier, "Arkansas Christian College" began in 1922 and in 1924, after the death of James A. Harding who inspired much of the work behind the school, was renamed "Harding College."

## Pepperdine

In 1937 George Pepperdine, founder of Western Auto Stores, used his fortune to start a school on the West coast in California, which after him, was name "George Pepperdine College."

## Others

Along with these more prominent and well-known colleges were several small schools: Pacific Christian College (1918); Montgomery Christian College (1942); Lubbock Christian College (1942); Florida Christian College (1946); Columbia Christian College (1949); Oklahoma Christian College (1950); etc.

# *Orphan Homes*

As early as 1909 brethren began building orphan homes with schools to care for and educate the fatherless and homeless. An understanding of these institutions and their support, as with the colleges, is important to grasp a sense of the controversies that began around 1950. Some of the homes operate under separate boards and others under local elderships.

The Tennessee Orphan Home (Spring Hill) began in 1909. Potter Orphan Home began in Bowling Green, Kentucky in 1914. Tipton Orphan Home began in 1921–22 and is in Tipton, Oklahoma. Boles' Orphan Home started in 1924 in Quinlan, TX. Ontario Children's Home was begun in 1929 in California. The Sunny Glen Home was founded in 1936 in Mercedes, Texas, in the Rio Grande Valley. Maude Carpenter Children's Home began in 1948 in Wichita, Kansas. The Shultz/Lewis Orphan home started in 1948 in Valparaiso, Indiana.

## *Sponsoring Cooperatives*

Almost from the inception of the missionary society brethren have sought to accomplish the goals of the society by functioning under the oversight of a centralized or sponsoring eldership.

### Texas

Soon after the civil war brethren in Dallas urged churches to cooperate through the eldership of a single church in support of preachers in destitute fields.

### Tennessee

In 1910 churches in West Tennessee began a cooperative effort under the eldership at Henderson, TN to support preachers in that part of the state.

### Ryman Auditorium

In 1922 many churches in Nashville, Tennessee, pooled their resources, talents, and efforts to conduct a centralized meeting at the old Ryman Auditorium. N. B. Hardeman was selected to be the speaker. Similar efforts were conducted in 1923, 1928, 1930, 1942 with Hardeman as speaker.

### Music Hall

A cooperative work of the Houston, Texas, churches in 1945 selected Foy E. Wallace Jr. to speak in the Music Hall Auditorium of that city on the general topic of Premillennialism. He did the same in 1946 on "Catholicism" and "Denominationalism." N. B. Hardeman conducted this meeting in 1947.

### Herald of Truth

What started as a cooperative radio program in Iowa blossomed into a national radio and TV program after 1952 when it was placed under the eldership of the Fifth and Highland Church in Abilene, Texas. Hundreds of churches soon poured millions of dollars into this program.

## *Debates*

Debates became a prominent tool and avenue through which preachers among Churches of Christ defended and propagated their views of "restoration."

## Baptist

Several debates were held with the Baptists over issues such as the necessity of baptism, the Spirit operating through the word, and the possibility of apostasy. Ben Bogard was the prominent Baptist debater of those years and had debates with most of the well-known debaters of the church—Joe Warlick, J.D. Tant, C.R. Nichol, A.G. Freed, N.B. Hardeman, etc.

## Christian Churches

Debates were also held occasionally in discussion of the missionary society and musical instruments in worship. Joe Warlick and Clark Braden discussed the music question as early as 1898; W. W. Otey and J. B. Briney debated both the society and the instrument question in 1908; N. B. Hardeman and Ira M. Boswell discussed the music question in 1923.

## Premillennialism

R. H. Boll began speculating on dispensationalism in the *Gospel Advocate* in 1911 and by 1915 had created much dissension over the theory. He and H. Leo Boles had a written debate in the *Advocate* in 1927. Foy E. Wallace, Jr., and Charles M. Neal had an oral debate on the issue in Winchester, KY in 1933.

## Others

Debates on these and many other topics were a way of life with gospel preachers and literally hundreds of discussions were held from 1900 onward. Joe Warlick is said to have had 399 debates; J. D. Tant and C. R. Nichol conducted more than 200 each.

# Controversy: A Summary of Issues and Division

## *Sunday School Literature*

A few brethren viewed Bible classes as "Sunday School Societies," paralleled them to the missionary society, and broke fellowship with churches who used this means to edify the church. They also made a distinction between oral comments in a class or sermon and comments in Bible study literature, concluding that written lessons were equivalent to creeds. These two issues created serious disruptions of fellowship in some parts of the country—mainly Texas, Arkansas, and Missouri. At one time there were about 200 preachers who defended these views.

## *Premillennialism*

A sizeable number of brethren and churches were influenced by the writings of R. H. Boll, E. L. Jorgenson, J. R. Clark, Charles M. Neal, and others who propagated the premillennial theory. A breach of fellowship was obvious by 1950. These brethren were strong in Louisville and other parts of Kentucky, southern Indiana, Louisiana, and Texas.

## *Institutionalism/Benevolence*

The issues that created the largest breach among the Churches of Christ revolved around questions concerning the autonomy and independence of local churches. Yater Tant lived through this controversy and has written a brief account of it as an addendum to Homer Hailey's book *Attitudes and Consequences of the Restoration Movement*. The following material is taken primarily from that source:

> In the mid 1930s the "College and Orphan Home" problem began to emerge as an issue which was destined eventually to rupture the unity of the "non–progressives" (Churches of Christ, LAS) as "restructure" had ruptured the unity of the "progressives" (Christian Churches, LAS). The Bible colleges have traditionally been hard pressed for funds, and there has always been a strong desire on the part of some advocates of the schools to solicit church support for such institutions. Ever since the days of Campbell, articles have appeared from time to time in the various religious journals suggesting that churches should make contributions to the schools. But the problem reappeared in 1947 when Abilene Christian College undertook to raise $3 million in an expansion program. Robert M. Alexander was put in charge of the fund–raising activities, and immediately began to campaign which was interpreted as an effort to secure church contributions to the colleges.
>
> The *Bible Banner,* edited by Foy E. Wallace Jr., and with such men as Cled E. Wallace, Roy E. Cogdill, W. Curtis Porter, C. R. Nichol, and R. L. Whiteside as regular contributors, quickly took up the challenge, voicing strong opposition to the churches becoming involved in the campaign. Defending the church contributions were G. C. Brewer, N. B. Hardeman, and others. Wallace had written articles in the *Gospel Advocate* as early as 1930 and in the *Gospel Guardian* in 1935, making his position clear that churches

should not support colleges. John T. Hinds, C.R. Nichol, and F.B. Srygley had also written in opposition to church supported colleges.

C.R. Nichol had written in 1933 contending that such financing of benevolent institutions was comparable to the support of a missionary society. Despite such occasional and sporadic articles, however, most churches were favorable to the idea, even though most of them actually were not making contributions to the few small orphanages that were then in existence. N.B. Hardeman saw a clear parallel between church support of an orphan home and church contributions to a college. So, he wrote, "Why will these brethren support an orphanage and fight the schools? The possible answer is that there are too many of our best churches that support the orphan home, and these brethren are afraid to attack them." Hardeman then wrote, "If the church can do part of its work (caring for orphans) through a human institution, why can it not do another part of its work (teaching the Bible) through a human institution?"

Hardeman pressed the point vigorously, contending "the orphan home and the schools stand or fall together." Support of one justified support of the other. There could be no logical or scriptural reason to support the homes and withhold the support from the schools.

Wallace acknowledged the parallel but contended that the homes "so not offer the threat or power or danger of domination that exists in the colleges." He went on, however, to extend the argument to embrace the Missionary Society: "if the church can do its benevolent work through a 'board of directors,' (a benevolent board), why not its preaching work or 'missionary work' through a board. And certainly, if the church can do its education work through a board of education (college, LAS), there can be no logical reason why the same church could not do its missionary work through a board of missions.'"[276]

## *Sponsoring Churchism*

The efforts to centralize the work of evangelism took on the form of many churches working through and under the oversight of one eldership.

---
276  Hailey, *Attitudes…*, p. 249–252.

After World War 2 great enthusiasm developed among the churches for evangelization in the countries where America had been at war—Germany, Italy, and Japan. This brought on much discussion as to how to best realize the common goal or objective.

## The Broadway Church in Lubbock

As early as 1943, when it became apparent that the tide of war was turning in favor of the allies, efforts were begun to create interest in reaching the enemy nations. In that year the Broadway Church of Christ in Lubbock, TX began to build a special fund for evangelism in foreign countries. The congregation began to solicit contributions from other churches to augment the special fund established through the contributions from its own members. The entire fund was to be administered by the Broadway elders in carrying forward the evangelization of Germany. This marks the first serious effort of "non–progressive" Churches of Christ to mount a viable alternative to the Missionary Society of the "progressive" churches. It was the beginning of the "Sponsoring Church Cooperative," and was a very logical extension and development of the ongoing controversy over church support of colleges and orphan homes. They were all logically tied together.[277]

## The Texas Plan Revived

In reality, the Sponsoring Church Cooperative was only a modern revival of the plan which had been developed in Texas following the Civil War, and which had finally been laid to rest mainly through the unrelenting opposition of David Lipscomb and his co–workers in the *Gospel Advocate*. This plan called for the accumulation of funds from many churches to be placed under a single control and direction of the elders of a single church, and to be administered by them in the support of gospel preachers. Dr. Carroll Kendrick, a Kentuckian who had migrated to Texas before the Civil War, gave the sponsoring eldership a name which he felt described its function. He called it a "Receiving, Managing, and Disbursing Evangelistic Committee."

A similar plan was introduced under the oversight of the elders of the Henderson, TN church in 1910. David Lipscomb said of the plan:

> Now what was that but the organization of a society in the elders of this church? The church leaders at Henderson constitute a board to collect and pay out the money and control the evangelists for the brethren of West Tennessee, and all the preachers are solicitors

---

277  *Ibid.*, p. 253.

for this work. This very same course was pursued in Texas several years ago. The elders at Dallas were made the supervisors of the work, received the money, employed the preachers, and directed and counseled them.[278]

## Herald of Truth

While many antagonistic forces and inner tensions had been developing among the "non–progressive" churches, the thing that finally ruptured its fellowship, apparently irrevocably, was the inauguration in the early 1950s of a nationally broadcast radio program bearing the name *Herald of Truth*. Originating in Iowa under the vigorous promotion of two young preachers, the program was moved to Abilene, TX in 1952 under the "sponsorship" of the Fifth and Highland congregation. The controversy over the orphan home and the sponsoring church for foreign mission work now widely publicized the idea of a "a sponsor," and the churches generally seemed willing to accept the arrangement as scriptural so long as it was done "under the eldership." But the very magnitude of the *Herald of Truth* began to create some uneasiness, and to raise some questions in the minds of many.[279]

The first writer to seriously question the scripturalness of the *Herald of Truth*, as it was promoted, was Robert H. Farish, who asked, "Does any individual or local congregation have the right to plan and promote a program larger than that individual or congregation can support? This is the thing that needs attention. More and more individuals and local congregations are planning super programs of work, which exceed the bounds of the possibilities of that individual or congregation, and then calling on 'the brotherhood' to support their programs … the work of the church is to be under the direction of the local eldership, but the work of the church which the eldership is to plan and direct is restricted to the resources of the local church."

Earl West, author of the *Search for the Ancient Order*, wrote, "Forty–two years ago (this reference point is the Henderson, TN plan of 1910 for the 'sponsoring church' to promote evangelism in West Tennessee) David Lipscomb, F. B. Srygley, E. A. Elam, and J. C. McQuiddy would have said this would have been 'a step in the wrong direction' and 'the organization of a society in the elders of a local church.'"[280]

For the next few decades, the issue was carried out through debates and writing in brotherhood journals. Much writing and words have been

---

278   *Ibid.*, p. 254.
279   *Ibid.*, p. 253–54.
280   *Ibid.*, p. 255.

expended over the differences over church-supported colleges, orphan homes, and sponsoring church arrangements for doing the church's work.

### Proponents

The papers of the *Gospel Advocate* and *Firm Foundation* devoted themselves to favoring church support of orphan homes and other benevolent institutions. They defended the sponsoring church arrangement in evangelism. Other than a series of sermons by Batsell Barrett Baxter in 1963, which were published in tract form, little public defense has been given to church support of colleges. Some colleges, however, have solicited that support via letters.

### Opponents

Between the 1950s and 2000 papers like *The Gospel Guardian, Preceptor, Truth Magazine,* and *Searching the Scriptures* opposed the support of benevolent or educational institutions and sponsoring church arrangements for evangelism.

### Debates

Many debates were conducted in the 1950s on both subjects by competent and sincere brethren. The most conspicuous are the Holt-Totty Debate in Indianapolis; the Porter-Woods debates in Indianapolis and Memphis; The Tant-Harper Debates in Lufkin & Abilene, TX; the Cogdill-Woods Debates in Birmingham and Newbern, TN. Probably a hundred or so debates have been conducted on these and similar topics.

### Division

By the 1960s division had already happened in many communities and cities, and it was inevitable that a major rupture was to occur nationwide.

# Division: The Separation into Three Distinct Groups

Brethren known as the "conservatives" or "antis," who have opposed church support of institutions, sponsoring church arrangements, and church support of social and recreational activities make up the smallest group of this latest division. No separate statistics are available for any of these groups.

Brethren known as "institutional" or "mainstream" brethren, who support and defend all these innovations, consist of two-thirds or three-quarters of the congregations known as "Churches of Christ," but they are further divided into two groups.

Among the "institutional" brethren are those who are more progressive, who not only defend all these practices, but who likewise question the interpretation of the Bible, seek fellowship with Christian Churches, and in general accept many denominational practices. The distinction between these latter two groups is not exactly drawn yet, but the latter will ultimately be the dominant party.

## Conclusion

The idea of "restoration," the subject of this book, is both a biblical and necessary concept if men are to please God. The problem, as has existed from the beginning of time, is that man's desires and will often get in the way of doing what God authorizes. As this study reveals, man's attitude toward God's silence has been the sticking and stumbling point that has already created division twice in the nearly 200 years of the effort toward "restoration."

Restoration is impossible when men do not understand Thomas Campbell's slogan and honor the biblical truth it states. "Where the scriptures speak, we speak; where the scriptures are silent, we are silent" is a truth written all over the pages of the Bible.

## Discussion

1. When was fellowship with Christian Churches seen to be impossible? Why is 1906 designated as the time of division? Did controversy and division end for churches of Christ in 1906? What, again, was the stumbling point in the restoration movement?

2. What major colleges were started by 1937? When was the first orphan home established? List some of the sponsoring church cooperatives supported by churches. Who were some of the prominent debaters? Who introduced premillennialism among the churches? When?

3. Name three important controversies among the churches since 1906. What issue created the largest breach? Who called for the support of the colleges by the churches? Who opposed it? What did one preacher say stands or falls together? If churches can support benevolent institutions what else can they support, according to Foy E. Wallace, Jr.? Who and how were sponsoring church arrangements introduced? What previous arrangements was this compared to? What sponsoring church arrangement became the cause of division? What prominent debates were held on these issues during the 1950s?

4. How many divisions were there? Briefly describe the view of each group.

5. What is necessary to please God? What has always been the sticking point of restoration? What is necessary if true restoration is to take place?

# APPENDICES

## The Churches of Christ
## After the Institutional Controversy

By Steve Wolfgang

# Publisher's Note

We hope you have enjoyed reading through brother Stauffer's material on the Restoration Movement. It has been our pleasure to put his writing into print. His teaching and preaching through the decades have inspired and instructed countless souls across our country and beyond. As you have seen, the last chapter covered by L.A. did a great job in detailing the historical events of the first half of the twentieth century, and he also added a summary of the history of the church after the institutional controversy of the 1950s and early 1960s.

Great change has continued to occur within the Church over the last 75 years. With brother Stauffer's permission, Spiritbuilding asked Steve Wolfgang, a notable scholar and historian regarding the institutional controversy, as well as a shepherd and evangelist for the Downers Grove church in Chicago, IL, to write an appendix detailing the changes and developments among mainstream and non-institutional churches throughout the last few decades of the twentieth century and the first two decades of the twenty-first. In the appendix he covers more recent developments inside the mainstream church, and some of the controversies that have evolved inside it regarding the change in focus and the outlook on the church. He also draws out the activities of the non-institutional churches and then closes with an outlook for the future. There is good material here, worth your time to read and consider. We highly recommend it to you as a supplement to Brother Stauffer's excellent work.

We also are encouraged by the "thaw" in relations between non-institutional and mainstream brethren and it is our prayer that as we proceed further into the twenty-first century our actions will reveal our commitment to practicing the unity Jesus called for in John 17.20–21.

November 1, 2023

Matthew Allen, Owner of Spiritbuilding Publishers

# Appendix I:

# Aftermath of the Institutional Controversy

## *By Steve Wolfgang*

Even while the "institutional" controversy still raged in some places, Abilene Christian College historian Bill Humble attempted to provide an objective view of the situation:

> The most serious issue that churches of Christ have faced in this century is church cooperation and 'institutionalism.' Led by Roy Cogdill, Yater Tant, and the Gospel Guardian, a substantial number of churches have come to oppose such cooperative programs of evangelism as the Herald of Truth and the homes for orphans and aged, as they are presently organized. During the past 15 years many debates have been held, churches have divided, and fellowship has been broken. This is the most serious division, numbers wise, that churches of Christ have suffered. Whether the division is final, or whether it can be healed, is yet to be determined.[281]

The preceding chapter outlined some dimensions of the division over church donations to various business enterprises and "sponsoring churches." Specifically, Biblical discussion of those matters included the following concepts, advanced by those in "NI" churches.[282]

1. That God has revealed in Scripture certain patterns for believers to follow in executing their collective duties in congregational work and worship (Hebrews. 8:5).
2. That these "binding" patterns are expressed in terms of (a) "generic" or "specific" statements or commands; (b) specific accounts of action, and (c) necessary conclusions or inferences drawn from Scripture (Acts 15).[283] [33]

---

[281] Bill Humble, *The Story of the Restoration* (Austin, TX: Firm Foundation, 1969), p. 74.
[282] Adapted from *The Simple Pattern*, a 2012 book of essays by L.A. Stauffer, Steve Wolfgang, Paul Earnhart, Bill Hall, Dan King, and Carroll Sutton, explains much about the controversy (pp. 17–19). Available on Kindle.
[283] See David Koltenbah, "The Three Methods of Argument to Establish Divine Authority and the Three Arguments in Acts 15 (Parts I–III)" *Truth Magazine* 11:10–12 (July, August,

3. That the general or more "generic" statements or commands allow differing optional or expedient ways of obeying those requirements, while specific statements or examples provide more restrictive instructions and do not authorize alternative procedures.
4. That the differences between "general and specific" can be detected, and distinguished from incidentals, or from a variety of expedient ways, by correctly following common sense hermeneutical principles.[34]
5. That the Scriptures enjoin upon Christians a broad range of individual duties, obligations and privileges which can be carried out in a variety of optional and expedient ways, that God may be glorified.
6. That, by contrast, the collective duties enjoined upon Christians in their collective congregational capacity, are fairly limited and consist of worshiping God through prayer, vocal music, proclamation of the gospel, and the first day of the week observance of the Lord's Supper and financial collection to enable the congregation to carry out its collective responsibilities in discharging its own edificational and teaching duties, assisting needy saints, and supporting preachers in their work of proclamation and teaching.
7. That, while some collective duties may overlap individual obligations (teaching, singing, prayer, for example), individual and collective (congregational) activities are not identical and can be easily and clearly distinguished one from the other.
8. That since collective activity, which requires a common mind, acceptance and agreement to common supervision (by elders, if qualified), and the pooling of financial resources is inherently fraught with possibilities of disagreement in matters of detail, it should be limited to those activities clearly enjoined upon Christians in acting together as a congregation, allowing room to respect the conscience of others, even of weak or untaught brethren (Romans 14).
9. That, in regard to preaching the gospel, Scripture reveals only that evangelism was accomplished by individual preachers, self-supported or remunerated by congregations (by example, directly, without the aid of some intermediary or "sponsoring" church, or "missionary society," whether called by that name or identified as a "steering committee" or other terminology—2 Cor. 11:8–9; Phil. 4:15–18).
10. That Scripture several times records churches assisted their own needy saints or sent funds for the temporary relief of congregations

---

September, 1967), pp. 234ff., 255ff., 275ff.; "The Apostles' Appeal to Scriptural Authority," in *Biblical Authority, Its Meaning and Application: Florida College Annual Lectures, 1974* (Fairmount, IN: Cogdill Foundation, 1974), pp. 80–94.

in "want,"—but that such relief was temporary, not sent from one prosperous church to another, and never for purposes of evangelism in which each congregation has equal obligations to the limit of its ability. Most conservatives have stressed the independence and autonomy of each local congregation, insisting that 20th century "sponsoring-church" conglomerates or other centralizing tendencies, no less than a missionary society or the Baptist associations and conventions, compromise New Testament principles regarding the nature of Christ's church.[35]

11. That the church Jesus died to purchase is a spiritual institution with a uniquely spiritual function and is therefore not to be remade into a hybrid welfare organization-country club responsible for alleviating social ills or for the entertainment of its members.
12. That human societies and institutions (colleges, orphanages, publishing companies, hospitals, etc.) which may be utilized as expedient means on a fee-for-service basis, am not be appended to the church and maintain their livelihood by church donations, and that all such attempts to make them parachurch or church-related institutions is foreign to the New Testament.[284]

The analysis by historian Bill Humble, quoted above, was written near the end of the "debating period" of the controversy. The note of cautious optimism struck here might have been due to the *Arlington Meeting*, held about the time Humble's book was written and in which he participated.[285] However, the positive tone produced by Arlington was short-lived. Another, less flattering description was recorded by Rubel Shelley of Freed-Hardeman College a year later:

> "While there are a few places where 'anti-ism' is still a real threat to the true faith, it is generally of no consequence. Isolated little groups of 'antis' still meet; but they are withering away and are having no appreciable effect on the brotherhood at large."

This analysis of the "antis" probably summarized a majority view in Churches of Christ toward "non-cooperation" or "non-institutional"

---

284 For more detailed explication of these concepts consult *Pursuing the Pattern*, a 2017 sequel to *The Simple Pattern*, with both persuasions represented from opposite perspectives of these issues, including Greg Tidwell (editor of the Gospel Advocate), Doug Burleson (Freed-Hardeman University), Buddy Payne (Florida College), Steve Wolfgang, Glenn Ramsey (who had debated L.A. Stauffer on these "issues") and others.
285 *The Arlington Meeting* (Orlando, FL: Cogdill Foundation, 1969). Arlington was a "model" for similar meetings occurring in Nashville (1988) and Dallas (1990).

churches.[286] Describing this "false doctrine" as "antagonistic to clear Bible teaching," Shelly contended that the typical "anti" usually "cut his own throat by his arrogant and malicious acts and statements" and was "quick to draw a line of fellowship and exclude himself from the larger portion of our brotherhood."[287]

This was not an isolated attitude. A decade later, the editor of the **Gospel Advocate** reiterated the "dying–on–the–vine" theme in an editorial in which he estimated that the "antis" composed 5% of churches of Christ and pleaded with them to "come back home . . . to the old paths . . . and preach again in the great churches," alleging that "anti doctrine cannot build great churches, inspire missionaries, and encourage pure and undefiled religion."[288] A well–known church–supported–college professor argued not long afterward that those who teach that Christians could "visit fatherless and widows by taking them in your home" have "taken the narrow, crooked pig–path of radicalism."[289]

Such comments were typical of a long train of caustic rhetoric that had continued for decades, such as: "Infidelity, agnosticism, and 'anti–ism' have much in common. None ever brought a helping hand or healing ministry to the unfortunate of earth living in want and misery. Nor have they ever built a home for homeless children or a hospital in which to minister to the sick."[290]

---

286 "Non-Institutional" churches (meaning those which believe there is no scriptural warrant for church sending contributions to human institutions such as colleges, orphanages, and other businesses, or supporting "sponsoring church" arrangements in which many smaller churches send donations to larger "sponsoring" churches which exercise "oversight" of evangelistic works, television programs, and other media) are often labelled with the short-hand acronym "NI."
287 Rubel Shelley, "Some Basic Errors of Liberalism," in *The Church Faces Liberalism: Freed-Hardeman College Lectures, 1970* (Nashville: Gospel Advocate Company, 1970), pp. 33–34.
288 Ira North, "Our Anti–Cooperation Brethren Should Come Back Home," *Gospel Advocate*, 121:19 (May 10, 1979), pp. 290, 294. Many have since noted that the list of "great churches" named by North had, just a few decades later, adopted "progressive" stances and policies such as instrumental music, women in public worship, etc.
289 Tom Holland, *Challenge of the Commission: Sermon Outlines from Acts* (Brentwood, TN: Penman Press, 1980), p. 20.
290 Gayle Oler, "No Soup," *Boles Home News*, March 25, 1954, p. 1.

# "Progressive Drift:" Accelerating Tendencies

By the late 20th century, however, fissures in the unity of institutional proponents became too obvious to ignore, and any semblance of unanimity among those who perceived themselves as "mainstream" Churches of Christ had vaporized. For some who began to think twice about centralized foreign evangelistic efforts "under the oversight" of a single large American church, an additional concern was the message preached (or often, not preached) by the "missionaries" receiving such support.[291] Furthermore, alarms began to sound about the accelerating drift of "progressive" elements in their ranks.

Practices demonstrating the "social gospel" aspects of institutional churches continued to evolve and accelerate.[292] The use of church buildings not just for fellowship dinners (justified as "love feasts") but also for "Scouts, quilting groups, exercise meetings, senior citizens, family reunions, receptions, and youth basketball and volleyball teams" in addition to "seminars on aging, divorce recovery, self-esteem, personal finances, stress and biblical exposition of books" were commonly accepted as though Biblical justified, without rebuttal or rebuke from editors or anyone else. The trek deep into social activities expanded to not-so-isolated incidents of secular adult education classes, English as a second language, and GED classes offered by the church; marriage and mental health counseling centers, medical-dental clinics, daycare centers, and among other things, job placement services. Brethren who might have been scandalized earlier in the "NI" controversy by the use of the church building for a "Chris Christian Concert" or a "Day at the Movies" (both with an admission fee) or a youth

---

291 In an interesting historical analogy, David Filbeck has ably demonstrated that much of the opposition to the centralized missionary society of the 20th-century Christian Churches was due to the diluted (even modernistic) message of those so supported; their concerns were as much or more about the message than about methods. David Filbeck, *The First Fifty Years: A Brief History of the Direct-Support Missionary Movement* (Joplin, MO: College Press Publishing Company, 1980), pp. 36–59. While the objections of some of the opponents of centralized missionary work among churches of Christ did not center around traditional "modernism," the heavy emphasis on the social gospel aspects of much "mission work" was a definite factor. See Otis Gatewood, *Preaching in the Footsteps of Hitler* (Nashville: Williams Printing company, 1960), pp. 72–75. Though defending his "relief works" in Germany, Gatewood acknowledged that "Problems arose as a result of such work, it is true. Some wanted to be baptized only to get food and clothing." Furthermore, "all this [distribution of food and clothing] took much time that could have been spent teaching the Bible" (pp. 70, 72).

292 For an interesting and still-relevant exchange on "social-gospelism" among churches of Christ, see J.W. Roberts, "What is the Social Gospel?" *Gospel Advocate* 104 (July 2, 1959), 419–420; and Ed Harrell, "Thoughts on Dishonesty," *Gospel Guardian* 11:20 (September 24, 1959), pp. 312–314; and Harrell, "The Social Gospel," *Gospel Guardian* 12:15 (August 18, 1960), pp. 225ff.

rally featuring the "World's Largest Hot Dog" all in the name of the crucified Christ, passed those milestones some time ago.[293]

The 1986 "Expression of Concern," signed by hundreds of preachers of the institutional persuasion (a virtual "Who's Who" of well-known veteran preachers among the "institutional mainstream" of Churches of Christ) published this bill of particulars reflecting alarm regarding theistic evolution issues and other situations at ACU, but also stating more general concerns:

"We are deeply disturbed over the liberalism that is so evident in the brotherhood today. By "liberalism" we mean especially the following items, though not excluding other specifics that could be mentioned:

> "A. There is a drifting from the Bible-centered, definitive, distinctive doctrine that once characterized our preaching. Presently, uncertain sounds and weak messages emanate from many pulpits among us. Brethren are becoming accustomed to diluted and polluted preaching. We are rapidly approaching the point where many of our people, including preachers and elders, no longer know the difference between true Christianity and the corrupted forms of it so prevalent about us.

> "B. There is a concerted effort on the part of some of our brethren to restructure the organization, worship, and work of the church along sectarian lines, thus tending to denominationalize the New Testament body of Christ.

> "C. A spirit of doctrinal compromise and fellowshipping of those in blatant religious error has permeated our ranks.

> "D. The world has made alarming inroads into the church. Instead of the church influencing the world for righteousness, as it should, the world has adversely affected many brethren in matters of morality and conduct of life.

> "E. The typical emphasis of the denominational world on recreation, entertainment, and solving the social ills of society has been incorporated into the thinking and programs of many congregations, supplanting the God-given work of meeting the desperate spiritual needs of those both within and without the body of Christ."[294]

No "anti" could have stated the case better. But the prominence of the signers made it impossible to dismiss the "expression of Concern" as merely the isolated carping of disgruntled "NI" brethren. Indeed, historians among institutional churches stated the obvious: "There was a time when Churches of Christ were widely known as a people of the Book. All who knew us knew that we hungered above all for the word of God. They knew that we immersed ourselves in its truths and sacrificed dearly to share the

---

293 For example, Douglas F. Parsons, "Increasing Church Visibility," *Gospel Advocate* 130:3 (March, 1988), pp. 24–25; *Ashwood Leaves* (Nashville, TN), February 2 & 9, 1986, and October 11, 1987; *Bering Today* (Houston, TX), July 1978.
294 *An Expression of Concern* (Ft. Worth, TX: Gospel Preachers, 1986). See also Roy Deaver, "Two False Extremes: Anti-ism and Liberalism," *Spiritual Sword* 16:2 (January 1985), p. 6; Thomas B. Warren, "Anti-ism Shackles the Church; Liberalism Opens the 'Floodgates' of Apostasy," *Spiritual Sword* 17:3 (April, 1986), p. 1.

gospel with those who had never heard. These were our most fundamental commitments. We knew it, and others knew it." These historians make a persuasive case documenting the drift as "American members of Churches of Christ have spiraled upward to a much higher socio-economic plane."[295]

Recollections by well-known older preachers whose preaching life spanned the 20th century vividly summarize the extent of change and drift. When asked to compare the church and its members in the 1980s to those of the 1930s, a former president of David Lipscomb College responded, "I don't think they see the glory of the church, unencumbered by denominationalism, as I did ... when I was growing up." Furthermore, he opined, "I don't think members of the church think the church is different from Protestantism. When I started preaching members of the church believed Protestants needed to be saved. We've lost a lot of that. It goes back to an understanding of the distinctiveness of the church. At an earlier time, they really felt the gospel was a lot better than Protestantism."[296]

A similar concurring opinion was expressed by the former head of the ACC Bible Department, Paul Southern. Noting that "one does not need to be a carping critic to recognize that the church is going through a crisis," Southern continued:

> Only a blind optimist with his head in the sand can deny what is obvious. Current conditions present an ugly picture. Apostasy has already begun in some congregations. Ecumenical fellowship is replacing church identity more and more ... Many sermons that we hear nowadays would be acceptable in almost any denominational pulpit. Denominational error is seldom, if ever, condemned.[297]

Richard Hughes' history of the evolution of Churches of Christ describes some of the changes which led to the "denominationalizing" of many of those churches.[298] Those who opposed what Hughes describes as a "fighting style" of preaching and writing by "focusing on various aspects of grace subtly transformed the long-standing tradition of tolerance for different viewpoints into a tradition of consensus. ..." Hughes observes that "over

---

295  C. Leonard Allen, Richard T. Hughes, and Michael R. Weed, *The Worldly Church: A Call for Biblical Renewal* (Abilene, TX: ACU Press, 1988); quotations from pp. 1–2, 6–7.
296  Robert E. Hooper and Jim Turner, *Willard Collins, The People Person* (Nashville: 20th Century Christian, 1986), pp. 116, 118.
297  Paul Southern, "Crisis in the Church," *Christian Journal*, Vol. XXXII, No. 2, April 1991, 2.
298  Quotations in the paragraphs which follow are from Richard T. Hughes, *Reviving the Ancient Faith: The Story of Churches of Christ in America* (Eerdmans, 1996), 193, 202.

the years the church's most progressive leadership proved more inclined to search for consensus than to undertake free and open discussions of different points of view. At the same time the progressives increasingly came to identify the old debating tradition fostered by Alexander Campbell and his heirs in the 19th century with intolerance. ..."

In their attempts to shape consensus, those who opposed the "fighting style" (quintessentially typified, in Hughes' view, by the preaching and writing of Foy E. Wallace, Jr.) increasingly "endeavored to build a consensus around positive and constructive themes and to eliminate negative themes altogether."[299] Indeed, re-stating what has become obvious to many observers (even while denied by some others), Hughes contends that "throughout the remainder of the century, this emphasis on positive thinking increasingly became a hallmark of the progressive leadership of Churches of Christ."

Furthermore, in a context of "preoccupation with consensus built on positive thinking," opponents of the "fighting style" determined that theological issues often generated considerable controversy:

> In the interest of harmony and consensus, therefore, they increasingly ignored the theological issues that had proved so divisive in the past and focused instead on biblically rooted cultural values that might serve as the basis for unity and peace—the practical value of providence and prayer, for example, and the values of family life, Christian unity, Christian business ethics, Christian education, kindness, goodness, basic morality, and the role of Christianity and promoting mental health.

Hughes' observations as a historian accord with the recollections of well-known older preachers who began preaching in the early 20th century. To cite only one example, G.K. Wallace, describing his earliest preaching days in the 1920s and 1930s from a perspective a half-century later, recalled: "Most of the baptisms were from the denominations. In those days denominational people would come to our meetings. ... Denominational people do not come these days to our meetings and if they did, they would not, in most places, hear anything that would lead them out of false doctrine."[300]

---

299  An illustrated biography of Foy E. Wallace which places him in historical context is Noble Patterson and Terry J. Gardner, *Foy E. Wallace: Soldier of the Cross* (Ft. Worth, TX: Wallace Memorial Fund, 1999).
300  G.K. Wallace, *Autobiography and Retirement Sermons* (High Springs, FL: Mary Lois Forrester, 1983), 17.

# "Electronic Bishops" and Changes in Preaching

The controversy over church-supported human institutions thus brought some profound, subtle (and not-so-subtle) changes in sermon content, style, and tone. In a climate of the positive-thinking, peace-of-mind agenda of much of the religious world, "messages that extolled the 'true church' and condemned 'the denominations' for their 'false doctrine' were not likely to develop a significant following beyond the ranks of the faithful." As historian Richard Hughes' described the situation:

> Churches of Christ found that they could not expect to compete effectively in the denominational free-market of souls unless they embraced the sort of peace of mind piety that had dominated the national religious landscape for more than a decade. ... With increasing frequency ... [the Herald of Truth] explained to national radio or television audiences how to achieve spiritual growth and peace of mind, how to develop healthy family relationships, and how to cope with anxiety and fear or with the various stages along life's way.[301]

Thus, the institutional controversy was not only about the doctrinal arguments regarding the biblical basis (or lack of it) for the manner of organization (channeling funds through and tying thousands of congregations together under the oversight of one church). It was also about the influence of the print and emerging electronic media—especially in changing the substance and content of the message preached. Furthermore, it created an entirely new source of "authority" for many in churches of Christ in altering the level of influence held by editors and print-media authors who had operated for two centuries under the assumptions implicit in the whimsical and oft-repeated dictum that Restoration-movement churches "do not have Bishops—they have Editors."[302] Hughes describes a particularly potent sort of "electronic bishop:"

> The "electronic bishops" did not so much speak to issues already established as they symbolically defined, by virtue of the issues they chose to address and those they chose to ignore, which issues

---

301 Hughes, *Reviving the Ancient Faith*, 241–242.
302 The influence of papers and editors is explored in some detail in Richard T. Hughes, Henry E. Webb, and Howard E. Short, *The Power of the Press—Studies in the Gospel Advocate, The Christian Standard, and the Christian-Evangelist: The Forrest F. Reed Lectures for 1986* (Nashville: Disciples of Christ Historical Society, 1986).

> were worth discussing and which were essentially irrelevant.... As the "electronic bishops" increasingly focused on issues pertaining to self-esteem, anxiety, marriage and the family, and the like, pulpit preachers ... quickly followed suit. By the 1970s ... *one could listen to preachers in Churches of Christ for weeks and months on end and never hear anything remotely approaching the message that had defined them for a century and a half* (italics mine—SW).[303]

Perhaps as important as any other aspect of the controversy is Hughes' insight that ironically, "the symbolic power of the 'electronic bishops' went largely unrecognized by all involved—by the 'bishops' themselves, by the elders of the Highland Church of Christ, by the multitude of congregations that supported the 'Herald of Truth' and even by the anti-institutional wing of Churches of Christ. Since Churches of Christ had historically denied the existence of any power that transcended the local congregation, no one was really prepared to appreciate the enormous power associated with national television programming." Irony abounds:

> Nonetheless, the "electronic bishops" effectively—and very quickly—defined themselves out of existence.... By the mid-1970s, *in fact, the message of the "Herald of Truth" had become indistinguishable from the messages being presented by a variety of other conservative and/or evangelical radio and television ministries.* And by then, many among Churches of Christ ... looked more to these evangelical ministries than to the "Herald of Truth" for intellectual and spiritual direction. Thus, it can be said the "electronic bishops" sowed the seeds of their own destruction. By the 1980s, they were gone. Few looked to "Herald of Truth" to provide theological leadership, and the "print media bishops" had long since passed from power. Little wonder, then, that Churches of Christ found themselves in considerable theological disarray.[304]

## Encroaching Evangelicalism

Other alterations in preaching style and substance among Churches

---

303 Hughes, *Reviving the Ancient Faith*, 242–243.
304 *Ibid.*, 244. For a perspective from one who was a speaker and active participant in Herald of Truth broadcasts, see *Every Life a Plan of God: The Biography of Batsell Barrett Baxter*. Baxter's PhD dissertation in communication from the University of Southern California analyzing changes and continuities in the themes of the Lyman Beecher Lectures on Preaching at Yale Divinity School from 1872–1944 was later published as *The Heart of the Yale Lectures* (New York: Macmillan, 1947; reprint, Baker, 1971).

of Christ are described by the late Pepperdine University professor of communication and rhetoric, Michael Casey (1954–2007)—citing some of the same impulses from the evangelical world and the broader American cultural shifts during the 1960s. During that decade, as the "institutional" controversy ended in most places, those who carried the day with most of the colleges, papers, and congregations began "another major transformation, as evangelical perspectives became increasingly popular." Various preachers and other leaders among Church of Christ "read, listened to, and attended conferences and meetings of David Wilkerson, Harold John Ockenga, and other evangelical leaders, and argued for the priority of evangelism in a more evangelical doctrine of the indwelling of the Holy Spirit." Along with the new evangelical theological emphases, ... other sympathetic younger preachers began to model preaching resembling that of evangelicals—more emotional and dramatic than typical preaching in Churches of Christ."[305] In this context, it became easy to dismiss those who would not agree to go along and get along and could be deemed expendable and shed from the "mainstream."

Using Max Lucado (described as "one of the best-known preachers and Christian authors in America") as an exemplar reflecting the influence of the changes in preaching style and substance wrought by the *Herald of Truth* and the "electronic bishops," Casey observes that Lucado "adapted the narrative capabilities of his mentor, Lynn Anderson" (one of the main *Herald of Truth* speakers). Noting that "narrative or storytelling is the primary technique in Lucado's preaching," Casey reported that "occasionally he has simply told a story for the entire sermon. Once he moved the pulpit out of the way and sat in a big chair and narrated a fable that he had written," noting that "the postmodern style of preaching is increasingly prevalent in both Church of Christ and in the wider evangelical world."[306]

By the 1990s, an increasing flood of illustrations signaling a drift from an insistence on biblical patterns, spawned an avalanche of protest. One such broadside was Goebel Music's mammoth book, *Behold the Pattern*, which adduced, at great length, cases ranging from the teaching of evolutionary

---

305 Michael W. Casey, "Preaching: Churches of Christ," *Encyclopedia of the Stone-Campbell Movement*, 608. Several of the themes excerpted in the paragraphs which follow are expounded in greater detail in Casey's *Saddlebags, City Streets, and Cyberspace: A History of Preaching in the Churches of Christ* (Abilene, TX: ACU Press, 1995).

306 Ibid., 608. A recent work analyzing the relationship of "restorationists" to evangelicalism is the collection of essays edited by William R. Baker, *Evangelicalism and the Stone-Campbell Movement* (Downers Grove, IL: Inter-Varsity, 2002).

theories at ACU to the Nashville Jubilee and the David Lipscomb University lectures, and much more, and identifying a cast of characters including Max Lucado, Rubel Shelly, Randy Mayeux, and many others.

> [I] do not see how there can be a single doubt in anyone's mind as to the fact that SOMETHING IS HAPPENING among us and to us as a people of God...I can safely say this, as if THE PATTERN is rejected by our preachers, elders, deacons, and members, then we can do or teach anything that we feel like we are "big enough" to do and or to teach. This is the case, for where there is no standard, no blueprint, no guide, no norm, no model, etc., then it is up to man to do what he desires and wants to do (cf. Judg. 17:6, 21:25). Sacred history reveals this happened ... [when every man] "did that which was right in his own eyes."[307]

Still, as with earlier efforts by some of these same preachers to correct and reclaim the Herald of Truth, which was seen as careening off the doctrinal rails under the guidance of a generation of younger preachers,[308] the "old guard" of the mainstream again found themselves outflanked and increasingly irrelevant in the eyes of a new generation of "seekers" who were shopping the market for some new thing.[309]

The trends emerging among the avant-garde of the Churches of Christ (at least, among those who had not already departed for greener pastures in the wider evangelical/denominational world) were aptly characterized by Michael Casey at the dawn of the 21st century:

> Increasingly, leading preachers turn to the language, props, and forms of television shows in narrating sermons. Popular television game show formats provide the form for the sermon content. Preachers become characters from popular television sitcoms, along with featured replica props, again to narrate ideas or create a dialogue with the congregation to convey the ideas of the sermons.

Casey's conclusion: "Preaching in rural and urban grace-oriented Churches

---

307 "A Potpourri of What's Happening" in Goebel Music, *Behold the Pattern* (Colleyville, TX: 1991), 622ff.
308 See the Xeroxed booklet, *Memphis Meeting With Representatives of Herald of Truth, September 10, 1973* (n.p., n.d); for context, see Wolfgang, "History and Background ..." in *The Simple Pattern*, 29–31.
309 For an extensive and insightful analysis of the diverging streams of thought in the institutional "mainstream" of the late-20th century, see David Edwin Harrell, *Churches of Christ in the 20th Century* (University of Alabama Press, 2000), pp. 176–218 ("The Mainstream Becomes a Divided Stream").

of Christ, and in some large suburban congregations, has transformed its focus from what Alexander Campbell called the 'gospel fact' to a 'user-friendly' gospel."[310]

## Sect, Denomination—or What?

Many observers have noted the continuing trends and changes among the "mainstream" Churches of Christ. Various prominent spokespersons within those churches seem quite willing to use aspects of a sociological "sect-to-denomination" transition to explain the increasing accommodation of denominational doctrines and behaviors evident among those churches.[311] A leading spokesman among such brethren describes the evolution to denominationalism this way: "Just when churches up and down the street are re–evaluating their denominational status and seeking to be more nondenominational, many among us are abandoning the goal of nondenominational Christianity and seeking to be more like other denominational churches.... *That we have become what we once despised is undeniable.*"[312]

The unabashed, even welcome, acceptance of newfound denominational status among a younger generation of "Church of Christ preachers" became too evident to be denied by anyone with eyes to see or ears to hear. In particular, the attraction of evangelical mega-churches for the younger preachers among the institutional Churches of Christ was especially strong, as acknowledged by a former lectureship director at Abilene Christian University: "Given the impressive results of seeker churches like Willow Creek and Saddleback, the pull to mimic their direction is nearly irresistible.... One need only read the classified ads of churches looking for ministers in the *Christian Chronicle* to see the influence of seeker models on

---

310 Casey, "Preaching …" in *ESCM*, (Eerdmans, 2004), p. 608. Some sense of the alarmed reactions to this post-modern style of preaching can be discerned in Dan Chambers, *Showtime! Worship in the Age of Show Business* (Nashville: 21st Century Christian, 1997).
311 For clarity bout the "sect-to-denomination" process, especially relative to "Churches of Christ," see Ed Harrell, *The Emergence of the Church of Christ Denomination*. Appearing first serially, and re-published many times since, this work is probably most easily accessible presently as a download at http://thecobbsix.com/wp-content/uploads/2016/01/Emergence-of-the-Church-of-Christ-Denomination.pdf
312 Rob McRay, "The Last Will and Testament of the Churches of Christ," in Leonard Allen and Lynn Anderson, eds., *The Transforming of a Tradition: Churches of Christ in the New Millennium* (Orange, CA: New Leaf Books, 2001), 44. The irony of the title will be evident to any student of "Restorationist" history; in the same volume, see also Jim Woodruff, "How Do You Spell Restoration?" (a chapter adapted from Woodruff's *A Church That Flies: A New Call to Restoration in the Churches of Christ* [Orange, CA: New Leaf Books, 2000]).

our thinking about evangelism."[313]

The concerns of the rapidly vanishing older generation of leaders among institutional brethren at the dawn of the 21st century was nowhere more cogently expressed than in a 2002 *Christian Chronicle* interview with the late Abraham Malherbe (1930–2012), then Buckingham Professor Emeritus of New Testament Criticism and Interpretation at Yale University. Malherbe, a native South African converted under the preaching of Eldred Echols, came to Abilene Christian College in the 1950s, and thence to Harvard University for graduate study. He returned to teach at Abilene from 1963–1969 before moving to Yale University in 1970. His credentials to address these issues are impeccable, and his comments arresting:

> Q: What are some of your concerns for our fellowship?
>
> A: My major concern is our cozying up to those evangelicals who put a premium on feeling at the expense of reason. This is not an indictment of all evangelicals, for there are differences among them. … Evangelical priorities and language have come to suffuse much of the preaching in our fellowship. That, combined with the style of preaching, common in all churches these days, that is narrative and anecdotal rather than expository, results in sermons that are as theologically thin gruel as are many of the so-called praise songs we sing. It seems that the goal of many services is to achieve an emotional response without imparting biblical knowledge. When the same, non-expository approach is followed in a church's Bible classes, any Restorationist nuance easily disappears.[314]

## Churches of Christ at the Dawn of the Millennium

In the years since Malherbe's interview, the pace of the developments he described has only accelerated. Perhaps the best recent summary of such changes is provided by Philip Sanders (the public face of the "In Search

---

313 Mark Love, "The Church that Connects at Calvary," in Allen and Anderson, eds., *The Transforming of a Tradition*, p. 144. Some of the generational conflicts between older and younger preachers in "institutional" churches are documented in Douglas A. Foster, Mel E. Hailey, and Thomas L. Winter, *Ministers at the Millennium: A Survey of Preachers in Churches of Christ* (Abilene, TX: ACU Press, 2000).
314 "A Conversation with Abraham Malherbe," *Christian Chronicle* 59 (February 2002), 20. Admittedly, hearing voices of concern and observing the handwringing of an older generation over how far a younger generation has taken the logical conclusions of the seeds of their own liberalism is astounding, if not bizarre.

of the Lord's Way," a multi-congregation "sponsoring church" television program of the Edmond, Oklahoma, church). Citing a "postmodern rejection of authority, the distrust of logic, the distaste for restoration hermeneutics, the denial of patterns in Scripture, and the questioning of inerrancy," Sanders notes that "many preachers do not preach error but will not preach against error," and describes the current situation as the 20th century progressed into the next:

> In recent years some have fallen away from the truth and have followed the thinking of the world. Postmodern leaders have urged numerous changes in the brotherhood. … These leaders by rejecting Biblical teaching have pointed churches to follow the mindset of our culture. They are pressing for instrumental music in worship, women in roles of leadership, the fellowshipping of adults who were only sprinkled as infants, worship teams, hand clapping and lifting of hands in our singing, and accepting same-sex activity …
>
> Some are clearly stating the church of Christ is a denomination. They no longer believe God set a pattern for how His church is to organize, to worship, or to come to salvation … They believe religious groups who believe false doctrines and practice human traditions are nonetheless faithful children of God, since they display the "Spirit's influence" in their lives…They no longer believe heresy is a reason for judging or the withdrawal of fellowship, since we all have imperfect knowledge. They deny the existence of absolute truth, a move designed to thwart the authority of God and of Scripture.[315]

---

315 Philip Sanders, "The State of Churches of Christ in America," *Affirming the Faith Seminar*, North MacArthur Church of Christ, 9300 N. MacArthur Boulevard, Oklahoma City, OK 73132, February 28, 2015.

Appendix 2

# The Post-Modernist Express into the 21st Century

## By Steve Wolfgang

As the 21st century dawned, "Churches of Christ" seemed to face an increasingly fragmented and divided future. Many of the 20th-century predictions and warning signs of rapid change seemed to be fulfilled—more rapidly than some had anticipated. Historian Ed Harrell described "the mainstream Churches of Christ" as being "in the midst of what some of their scholars are calling an 'identity crisis,' a time when they are seriously questioning the reasons for their own existence."[316] The *Global History* of "The Stone-Campbell Movement" observed that "While a broad middle remained in the 1990s, 21st century Churches of Christ reflected a clear bifurcation between conservatives and progressives."[317] Perhaps historian Douglas Foster was nearer the truth in describing "our diversity and fragmentation" created by "a constant barrage of contradictory messages from the increasingly different institutions" and centers of influence in various quarters.[318] Progressives emphasized what they defined as "grace" over what they perceived as "legalism," promoting changes in worship (including instrumental music) and in hermeneutics, the inclusion of women in worship and leadership, social ministries, racial justice, and fellowship with other denominations—all of which sharply contrasted with the "exclusivism" often seen in more "traditional" Churches of Christ.[319]

---

316 Ed Harrell, "How My Mind Has Changed, *Christianity Magazine,* 8:10 (October 1991), p.32.
317 D. Newell Williams, Douglas A. Foster, and Paul M. Blowers, eds., *The Stone-Campbell Movement: A Global History* (St. Louis: Chalice Press, 2013), 230. This work highlights some of the diversity within Churches of Christ, including non-institutional, Black, one-cup, and non-class groups in various sections of the book.
318 Douglas A. Foster, *Will the Cycle Be Unbroken?: Churches of Christ Face the 21st Century* (Abilene: ACU Press, 2007), 66.
319 See Gregory Alan Tidwell, "Ten Trends Revisited," *Gospel Advocate* 161, no. 6 (June 2019): 24. As can be seen in this opening paragraph, labeling and buzzwords such as "legalism" and "grace" or "exclusivism" or "traditionalism" have been abundant—if not always accurate.

# Becoming Evangelical-Friendly

Historian Richard Hughes observed that as restorationists began to "adopt a more respectable 'denominational' status ... they almost invariably tend to adopt evangelical modes of self-definition."[320] The impact of Evangelical culture on Churches of Christ was filtered through the "praise songs" of contemporary Christian music (CCM), evangelical speakers and writers, increasing attendance at evangelical gatherings such as Promise Keepers, and megachurches such as, for instance, Willow Creek, Saddleback, or Southeastern Christian Church in Louisville. While varied, depending on particular situations, Evangelicalism's impact on Churches of Christ identity was broad and deep in many places and diverse ways.[321]

## "America's Best Preacher"

At the vanguard of leaders in Churches of Christ who influenced, and were influenced by, evangelical subcultures, Max Lucado serves as an obvious case study. In a six-page 2004 article for the flagship evangelical magazine *Christianity Today*, Lucado was styled "America's Pastor ... much in the tradition of Norman Vincent Peale or Billy Graham." The following year, *Reader's Digest* called Lucado "America's Best Preacher."[322] By 2004, Lucado's books had sold 33 million copies in 30 languages; by 2022, that number had soared to 120 million in 54 languages. Often compared to evangelicals such as Billy Graham, C.S. Lewis, Chuck Colson, Beth Moore, or Philip Yancey, articles by or about Lucado appeared in *Christianity Today* every year in the 21st century.[323]

The impact of evangelicalism and the broader denominational world

---

320  Richard T. Hughes, "Why Restorationists Don't Fit the Evangelical Mold; Why Churches of Christ Increasingly Do," reprinted as Chapter 6 in *The Grace of Troublesome Questions: Vocation, Restoration, and Race* (Abilene: ACU Press, 2022).
321  See Edward P. Myers, "Churches of Christ (A Cappella): Are We Evangelical?," in *Evangelicalism & the Stone-Campbell Movement*, ed. William R. Baker (Downers Grove: IVP Academic, 2002), 50–67, as well as other chapters in that work. For broader developments in Evangelicalism that incorporate the involvement of Churches of Christ, consult two significant works on American religion in the twenty-first century: highlighting connections of Churches of Christ and the Religious Right were Darren Dochuk, *From Bible Belt to Sunbelt: Plain-Folk Religion, Grassroots Politics, and the Rise of Evangelical Conservatism* (New York: W. W. Norton & Company, 2012), and Bethany Moreton, *To Serve God and Wal-Mart: The Making of Christian Free Enterprise* (Cambridge: Harvard University Press, 2009).
322  Cindy Crosby, "America's Pastor," *Christianity Today*, March 2004, 58–63.
323  Max Lucado website, https://maxlucado.com/about-max/.

seemed obvious when the Oak Hills Church of Christ in San Antonio, where Lucado had preached for many years, dropped "of Christ" from their name to become simply the "Oak Hills Church." According to Lucado, the name "Church of Christ" had become an "insurmountable barrier" to some people. Lucado also adopted evangelical views of salvation, rejecting baptism for the remission of sins as part of a "plan of salvation" in favor of evangelical versions of salvation as expressed in the sinner's prayer.[324] It is indicative of the identity crisis that the best-known minister among Churches of Christ in the 21st century was no longer known as a "Churches of Christ minister" but rather an evangelical-style pastor of a congregation that dropped any claim to being a "Church of Christ." Other "progressive" churches followed in the wake.

Various institutions followed suit. The *Christian Chronicle*, a newspaper-style publication seeking to inform readers about a broad spectrum of Churches of Christ, contained frequent articles about various denominational authors who, with increasing frequency, were welcomed, promoted, and proudly advertised among Churches of Christ, especially at the colleges they supported. Pepperdine University, Abilene Christian University, and other Church-of-Christ-supported schools invited progressive evangelical leaders such as Brian McLaren, Francis Chan, Rachel Held Evans, Dallas Willard, Scot McKnight, Esau McCaulley, and Biblical scholars such as Walter Brueggemann to speak.[325]

## Musical "Styles" and Instrumental Music

Additionally, Oak Hills Church added instrumental music to some of their worship gatherings.[326] By the early 2020s, many had followed Oak Hills' example—including "the nation's largest Church of Christ" at Richland Hills in Ft. Worth, where Rick Atchley preached.[327] Other prominent churches such as Otter Creek in Nashville, where various faculty at David Lipscomb University served as elders and church leaders,[328] were followed by many

---

324  Crosby, "America's Pastor," 62.
325  See, for instance, the ACU site https://www.siburtinstitute.org/summit-history
326  The December 15, 2005 *Baptist News* website reported Oak Hills and other congregations in Dallas and Seattle had adopted instrumental music. https://baptistnews.com/article/some-churches-of-christ-re-examine-tradition-of-instrument-free-worship/
327  The January 1, 2007 website of the *Christian Chronicle* reported, "Nation's largest Church of Christ adding instrumental service" (https://christianchronicle.org/nations-largest-church-of-christ-adding-instrumental-service/)
328  Heidi Hall, *Nashville Tennessean*, "Church of Christ opens door to musical instruments" (USA Today, March 6, 2015.

other smaller congregations in Dallas, Lubbock, Seattle and elsewhere.[329] These congregations often adopted variations of evangelical identity, deeply shaped by books like Lucado's.

As more progressive churches adopted instrumental music, institutions followed. By 2013, Abilene Christian University had added instrumental-music chapel services. An editorial in the ACU newspaper, the Optimist, reported "Immersed Chapel on Thursdays is an instrumental program that attracts a huge crowd every week. It is clear the majority of ACU students have no problem with instrumental music, in fact, many encourage it. Many small group Chapels also successfully utilize instruments in their services."[330]

In 2018, a *Directory of Churches of Christ* listed 60 congregations that used instruments in some or all gatherings.[331] Although those who use instruments are as yet a small minority of all "Churches of Christ," three of the five largest congregations listed in the 2018 *Directory* had dropped "of Christ" from their name and added instruments to at least some of their gatherings.

But while one of the most obvious such alterations among "institutional" Churches of Christ is the tremendously divisive controversy still raging over "worship styles" and the increasing demand for professional-quality music, including the instrumental variety, that issue may not be the most profound change occurring in 21st-century Churches of Christ. As many have observed, the adoption of instrumental music in worship may be only the proverbial tip of the iceberg. In the words of a widely respected older preacher among institutional churches, "instrumental music only lets the cat out of the bag. … After they bring in the instrument, baptism

is no longer essential, and the church is just another denomination among denominations."[332]

---

329  "Churches of Christ debate adding instrumental music to worship services," *Lubbock Online*, May 30, 2012; see also Nancy De Gennaro, "Local Church of Christ adds instruments to worship," (*Daily News Journal*, Murfreesboro, TN, April 16, 2015; https://www.dnj.com/story/life/2015/04/16/local-church-christ-adds-instruments-worship/25891291/)
330  See Editorial by the Optimist Editorial Board, "Instrumental music should be allowed," in the ACU newspaper The Optimist (October 18, 2013; see https://acuoptimist.com/2013/10/instrumental-music-should-be-allowed/
331  Carl Royster, ed., *Churches of Christ in the United States 2018*, (Nashville: 21st-Centry Christian), ix, 20.
332  Charles Hodge, "Facing the Instrumental Music Question Again," *Gospel Advocate* 140

# Women in Leadership Roles

Indeed, the most divisive issue among "progressive" churches in the 21st century may not be instrumental music, but rather the expansion of the roles for women in public ministry. Although some hint of what was to come may be seen in articles in *Mission Journal* in the 1970s,[333] by the time another generation had come to positions of decision-making capacities in churches and church-supported institutions in the 21st century, women graduates of theology programs in various Christian Colleges were serving as "preaching ministers" and other public roles in various congregations.[334] Pepperdine University advertised the appointment of a woman as University Chaplain in 2015—the same year Pepperdine featured a tattooed lesbian Lutheran preacher, Nadia Boles-Weber (who reportedly had grown up in a Denver-area "Church of Christ") as a keynote speaker on their Annual Lectureship.[335]

By 2021, fluid and growing registry of churches that included women in public worship (such as "leading prayer, giving communion talks, leading singing,…reading scripture, announcements, serving communion, etc.") listed about 100 congregations (out of nearly 12,000) which allowed women

---

(February 1998), 24. See also LaGard Smith, *Who Is My Brother? Facing a Crisis of Identity and Fellowship* (Malibu, CA: Cotswold, 1997), and the reaction in Wayne Jackson, *A Friendly Review of LaGard Smith's Who Is My Brother?* (Stockton, CA: Courier Publications, 1998). Note pp. 20–21.

333  See, for example, the March 1975 issue of *Mission*, (Volume 8, #9), "Women In Christ Today," featuring articles such as "God's Design; Women's Dignity" by Bobbie Lee Holley, "Women in Submission" by Pat Suba, "Women In Christ Today—A Seminar," by Marquita Moss; and other articles and commentary in subsequent issues, which reported an Austin, Texas seminar on women in Churches of Christ (and, perhaps not coincidentally, a 1974 Chicago conference on "Evangelical Feminism"). In some ways, similar themes and concerns addressed in the 20th-century print magazine *Mission* are reflected in the 21st-century digital *Missio Dei: A Journal of Missional Theology and Praxis*, begun in 2010 and edited by Greg McKinzie, who receive his PhD from the evangelical Fuller Theological Seminary; see https://missiodeijournal.com/issues/md-1/authors/md-1-mckinzie

334  Consult the gender-inclusive website http://www.wherethespiritleads.org/gender_inclusive_churches.htm for a listing of dozens of "Churches of Christ" featuring congregations all over the US which allow increasing (often full) participation by women in public worship roles. The website states that it not only promotes "Gender Equality and Inclusion n The Churches of Christ" but that "it is also intended for all Christian churches who practice gender restrictions, exclusion, and discrimination."

335  See "Bolz-Weber's liberal, foulmouthed articulation of Christianity speaks to fed-up believers," *Washington Post,* November 3, 2013; see also "Nadia Bolz-Weber is baffled by how churches became so squeaky clean," *Washington Post,* via Religion News Service, October 19, 2015.

in such participatory roles.[336] Of all Churches of Christ in the U.S., about 40 were open to women preaching—whereas about 60 congregations included instrumental music in their gatherings.[337]

The Boston–area Brookline church was an early pioneer in incorporating women in prominent ministry positions, and by 2021 had hired Candace Nicolds, who received a Master of Divinity degree from ACU, as "lead pastor."[338] Former Pepperdine University chaplain D'Esta Love, who also held an M.Div. from ACU, compiled a collection of 29 sermons by women in the Churches of Christ, many who later preached on the PreacHer podcast.[339] Some aspects of the inclusion of women in ministry among progressive Churches of Christ are chronicled by Sara Barton, who became Pepperdine University Chaplain in 2016, in addition to preaching regularly at the Camarillo, California, Church of Christ.[340]

For others, however, women's ministries among even progressive Churches of Christ proved too restrictive, and following a pattern reminiscent of a similar exodus to the Disciples of Christ and other denominations a century earlier, many women seeking to become preachers eventually departed for less constrained environs in the wider denominational world.[341] A

---

336 See *A Directory of Gender Inclusive and Egalitarian Churches in the Church of Christ Heritage;* Matt Dabbs, "Women's Roles in Churches of Christ Survey 2016," Wineskins.org, May 24, 2016, https://wineskins.org/2016/05/24/womens-roles-in-churches-of-christ-survey-2016/.

337 Even so, the annual gathering of the "Community of Women Ministers" seems to be growing, and was scheduled to meet during the 2023 ACU "Summit" lectureship (https://www.siburtinstitute.org/summit–schedule–fall–23). The 2023 Christian Scholars' Conference, held at the Lanier Theological Library in Houston, in collaboration with Lipscomb University, convened a panel on "Female Leadership in Churches of Christ." For more general information, consult "Gender Inclusive and Egalitarian Churches of Christ," Where the Spirit Leads, March 8, 2021, http://wherethespiritleads.org/gender_inclusive_churches.htm.

338 Brookline church website: http://www.brooklinechurch.org/public–worship

339 D'Esta Love, ed., *Finding Their Voices: Sermons by Women in the Churches of Christ* (Abilene: Abilene Christian University Press, 2015). The PreacHer podcast, begun in 2019 by Jennifer Hale Christy, a D.Min. graduate from Lipscomb University included, by 2022, more than 50 sermons in Churches of Christ by about 30 different women. See Jen Hale Christy, "Welcome to PreacHer! with Dr. Jen Hale Christy," May 15, 2019, https://podcasts.apple.com/us/podcast/preacher/id1463893859.

340 Sara Gaston Barton, *A Woman Called: Piecing Together the Ministry Puzzle* (Abilene: Leafwood Publishers, 2012). The book was praised by evangelical advocates such as Rachel Held Evans and Shane Claibourne, and by Churches of Christ leaders Rubel Shelly, Randy Harris, and Mike Cope.

341 See blogs by Kelly Edmiston on Scot McKnight's *Jesus Creed* blog, including "Leaving

revealing article from that prior controversy provides some insight into the broader hermeneutical conflicts involved in the evolution of the Disciples' modernistic mentalities (see Chapter 12, pp. 86–90). While focusing on an expanded public role for women in churches, the same expansive hermeneutical principles also allowed 19th–century progressives to accommodate a wide range of controversial issues, from instrumental music to the so–called "higher criticism" of scripture:

> A principle may set aside an apostolic precept. It may brush aside an apostolic decree. We do that constantly. We follow the apostolic example whenever we like it; when we do not, we depart from it.[342]

Indicative of such broadening hermeneutical perspectives, for example, Nashville's Otter Creek Church declared as part of their Vision 2029: "to become a more inclusive and diverse community of believers, we want to consider gender and race along with giftedness in hiring decisions for ministers and staff."[343] But even in progressive congregations like Otter Creek, achieving agreement for women to serve as elders remained elusive.[344]

---

(My) Church," *Jesus Creed* blog, October 9, 2019, https://www.christianitytoday.com/scot-mcknight/2019/october/leaving-my-church-by-kelly-edmiston.html; "Kelly Edmiston and Women in the Churches of Christ: Who Gets to Speak into That Microphone?," *Jesus Creed* blog, March 4, 2020, https://www.christianitytoday.com/scot-mcknight/2020/march/kelly-edmiston-and-women-in-churches-of-christ.html; Kelly Edmiston, "Fundamentalism in the Churches of Christ," *Jesus Creed* blog, March 11, 2020, https://www.christianitytoday.com/scot-mcknight/2020/march/fundamentalism-in-churches-of-christ.html; and Kelly Edmiston, "The 'New' Clergy in the Churches of Christ," *Jesus Creed* blog, March 18, 2020, https://www.christianitytoday.com/scot-mcknight/2020/march/new-clergy-in-churches-of-christ.html

342 George T. Smith, "No Man Wishes Women to Keep Silence in the Churches," *Christian Standard* 29 (October 7, 1893), p. 798. David Edwin Harrell, Jr., documents numerous examples of such reasoning in *The Social Sources of Division in the Disciples of Christ, 1865–1900* (Atlanta: Publishing Systems, Inc., 1973), especially chapters 1 and 13 (Harrell notes in the Preface that "the first and last chapters, taken together, are an interpretive essay on the sociological development of the church").

343 "Otter Creek Church Vision 2029," page 7, pdf available at https://ottercreek.org/what-we-believe/.

344 One exception was the Highland church in Abilene, long known as the sponsoring church for the Herald of Truth television program for much of the 20th century. In 2021, though with some dissent and loss of membership, the Highland elders announced to the congregation that the elders believed "Scripture makes a positive case for inviting spiritually gifted women to serve as elders" (https://pepperdinebiblelectures.podbean.com/e/an-inside-perspective-on-discernment-of-women-in-leadership/)

# A New Hermeneutic

A significant example of the interpretive journey followed by some who were transitioning from gender-exclusive to gender-inclusive viewpoints was the book *Women Serving God*, self-published in 2020 by John Mark Hicks of David Lipscomb University. Providing a window into the hermeneutics of progressive Churches of Christ, Hicks guided his readers down a path of increasing dissatisfaction with traditional positions on Biblical passages regarding the roles of women in worship gatherings, evolving from "limited" to "full" participation, contending that God equally "gifts" women and men and to participate in congregational worship.[345]

An earlier self-published work by the same author, *Searching for the Pattern*, provides some insight into the shifting perspectives involved in a trek from "traditional" to more progressive/permissive positions. Readily acknowledging that "rigorous application" of principles of Bible study "warranted the conclusion" on a given point of application involved in the controversy over church-supported human institutions, Hicks then argued:

> On the other hand, that conclusion did not sit well with me. Something gnawed at me. It was as if I felt that can't be right. And yet I knew that the heart is deceitful above all things, and I could not trust my feelings when it came to what the Bible taught. What the Bible said was true whether I liked it or not. Nevertheless, something seemed amiss.[346]

As the narrative continues, Hicks does exactly what he says he knows should not be done—privileging feelings over the often-challenging clarity of Scripture—all the while acknowledging the warnings and caveats about the dangers inherent in choosing that path. Following one's "gut" and favoring sentimentality and emotionalism over what one acknowledges to be Biblical teaching is a well-worn corridor leading to many permissive possibilities.

## "Non-Institutional" Churches

As the 21st century dawned, predictions and observations about "NI"

---

345 John Mark Hicks, *Women Serving God: My Journey in Understanding Their Story in the Bible* (John Mark Hicks, 2020). Other aspects of the hermeneutics of progressive Churches of Christ include Tom Olbricht, Jack R. Reese, *At the Blue Hole: Elegy for a Church on the Edge* (Grand Rapids: Eerdmans, 2021), p. 30. Leonard Allen, *In the Great Stream: Imagining Churches of Christ in the Christian Tradition* (Abilene: ACU Press, 2021), pp. 215, 223.
346 John Mark Hicks, *Searching for the Pattern: My Journey in Interpreting the Bible* (John Mark Hicks, 2019), p. 62; see also pp. 88–89.

churches abounded. Leroy Garrett's history, produced by a Christian Church publisher, even while noting that "anti" churches "have been particularly missionary in recent years," still projected that they were making "steady progress toward extinction."[347] Other historians saw different evidence of growth, not least from dissidents in increasingly progressive churches who defected to more conservative NI churches (just as many in Christian Churches quit the leftward-drifting churches in the 1930s to affiliate with non-instrumental churches"). Douglas Foster noted that "Leaders in the anti-institutional churches are calling conservatives in "liberal" mainstream churches of Christ to come over to them, and with some success."[348]

But such expansion did not come without its own version of "growing pains." As Ed Harrell pointed out, "As church growth accelerated and congregations multiplied, warnings about changing attitudes and doctrinal laxity could hardly be dismissed as figments of [anyone's] imagination."

Differences regarding issues including divorce and remarriage and attendant fellowship issues created considerable controversy, yet "for all the fussing and fighting at the end of the century, people in non-institutional churches uniformly looked backwards for examples and authority," as Harrell observed, "intent on grounding arguments in Scripture and willing to engage in honorable exchange." Still, as a historian Harrell could detect that "the profile of noninstitutional Churches of Christ was changing" and "as in the years before World War II, those changes did signal the appearance of sociological and ideological differences within the movement."[349] At the dawn of the digital age, "noninstitutional" churches seemed to be on a trajectory shadowing aspects "mainstream" Churches of Christ two or three generations earlier.

Ironically, one of the clearest ways to demonstrate the development and significance of NI churches may be through the parachurch institutions supported by individuals in those churches.

Florida College, in suburban Tampa, is an accredited four-year college which has existed for decades without soliciting or accepting contributions from churches It is patronized largely by members of churches of Christ which oppose such church support of institutions. Current enrollment is nearly 600 students from 33 states and 12 other countries.

---

347 Leroy Garrett, *The Stone-Campbell Movement: The Story of the American Restoration Movement* (Rev. ed; Joplin, MO: College Press, 1994 [5th Printing, 2006]), p. 435.
348 Foster, *Will the Cycle Be Unbroken?* p. 56.
349 Harrell, *Churches of Christ in the 20th Century*, pp. 358–359.

Subscription journals underwent radical changes in the digital age, especially post-Covid. The largest of these, issued monthly, were *Christianity* and *Searching the Scriptures* with about 6500 and 5500 subscribers, respectively, ceased publication by the turn of the century. *Truth Magazine*, which was the last of the print journals, transitioned to all-digital, online publication during the Covid pandemic, with a subscription list of about 3500.

The Foundation which publishes *Truth Magazine* also publishes books, tracts, and Bible class literature, a new hymnal (*Psalms, Hymns, and Spiritual Songs*) and a nearly complete set of New Testament (as well as several installments of a projected Old Testament) commentary sets. Since 1986 the Foundation has operated the CEI bookstore in Athens, Alabama, recently consolidating operations by selling its long-time location in Bowling Green, Kentucky, to OneStone Bookstore just as Religious Supply Center in Louisville, Kentucky, closed its operations. Spiritbuilding Publishers in Dayton, Ohio, continues as a mail-order supplier, and a few other journals, previously published as monthly or quarterly print publications with smaller subscription lists, have transitioned to digital publication in a fast-moving electronic age. Various individuals and groups also publish a variety of Bible class workbooks, tracts, hymnals, self-published books, and other Bible-related materials.

Although most churches of the non-institutional persuasion obviously do not participate in evangelistic projects such as Herald of Truth, many of their evangelistic efforts have been refocused to Internet-based studies, podcasts, or arrangements using Skype or other electronic/digital means of propagating the gospel. In overseas evangelism, non-institutional churches have usually opted for other means than sending American "missionaries" overseas for extended periods (though non-institutional churches have supported such men, and their families, in long-term efforts in Mexico, Canada, England, Ireland, Norway, Germany, Colombia, Chile, Argentina, Australia, Japan, the Philippines, the People's Republic of China, South Africa, and elsewhere). Frequently foreign nationals have been brought to the U.S. for a period of study and then supported for a period in their native culture by American churches. Other native preachers converted (either by Americans or foreign nationals trained in America) and working in their own culture are supported directly by American churches—a fairly high percentage of non-institutional churches have financially supported men engaged in various aspects of overseas evangelism.

Obviously, churches of the non-institutional persuasion do not donate financially to benevolent institutions; instead, they have "practiced what they preached" and provided such care individually. In 1965, Eugene Britnell surveyed 60 preachers who opposed church support of institutional orphan homes and accumulated a list of 450 orphans and widows cared for by such Christians ("Our Defense to Those Who Falsely Accuse Us"). In documentation assembled for the *Willis-Inman Debate* (1966), Cecil Willis gathered information demonstrating that 17 children had been adopted or cared for by the faculty at Florida College, which at that time consisted of about 25 families; and that the eight families represented by the editorial staff of the *Gospel Guardian* had provided homes at one time or another for at least ten children who were not the natural offspring of those families.[350] Currently, several individually-supported organizations such as "Sacred Selections," or "Help A Neighbor," and others, exist to enable individual Christians to cooperate in a number of benevolent enterprises and situations.

## A Thaw in Relationships?

According to statistics reported by Phillip Sanders, (host of the "In Search of the Lord's Way" —a multi-congregation "sponsoring church" television program of the Edmond, OK church), "NI" churches now compose 23% of "Churches of Christ"—compared with 54% classified as "Mainstream," and approximately 20% categorized as "Progressive."[351] The current "status" of NI churches, and the continuing basis of fundamental core beliefs have been explicated elsewhere in some detail.[352] One recent result of the controversies

---

350  This is perhaps also the place to notice that a reading of the *Gospel Advocate* and *Firm Foundation* for 1958–1962 demonstrates that the "institutional" brethren came very near fragmenting themselves over whether orphanages could be organized under a corporate board or must be overseen directly by elders of a church.

351  Philip Sanders, "The State of Churches of Christ in America," Affirming the Faith Seminar, North MacArthur Church of Christ, Oklahoma City, OK 73132, February 28, 2015. Perhaps the best way to interpret this estimate realistically is if one considers the shrinkage of the total number of all those identifying as "Churches of Christ" due to a number of churches no longer identifying as such. For an analysis of exit interviews of those leaving Churches of Christ in the 21st century, consult Flavil Yeakley, *Why They Left*. Differing perspectives are offered in Benjamin Williams, ed., *Why I Stayed: Honesty and Hope in the Churches of Christ* (2018), in which several contributors explain how and why they were willing to remain in particularly 21st-centruy "progressive" churches, rather than being ousted or departing voluntarily as often happened in an earlier era (as, for instance, described in the 20th-century screed, Voices of Concern: Critical studies in Church of Christism, ed. Robert Meyers (St. Louis:Mission Messenger, 1966). At a certain point, dissidents no longer feel pressure to leave an achieve some level of comfort in staying.

352  In particular, see Steve Wolfgang, "History and Background," 17–19, 24–27. For

between "progressives" and more "traditional" mainstream churches described by Sanders has been a renewed interest by some "institutional conservatives" in discussing differences with "non-institutional" brothers.[353] While one may applaud the thaw in relationships (given the chilled nature of disinterest between "NI" and "I" churches in recent decades), there are many among the shrinking "mainstream" who still view the dreaded "antis" as equally apostate as the left-wing "progressives."[354]

So, while one can appreciate the change in room temperature (neither frozen nor overheated), it appears that things are still "stuck at 1957" or so, given that fundamental differences still exist.[355] The situation seems analogous to what Jack P. Lewis reports regarding congenial "instrumental music brethren:"

> My contacts with instrumental people have not suggested to me that they are interested in giving up the instrument for fellowship purposes ... Rather, they are interested in acceptance while continuing their practice. In other words, they want what someone has called 'individual choice'—those who want the instrument can

---

another perspective on such matters, see Harrell, *Churches of Christ in the 20th Century*, chapter 7, and sections in Hughes, *Reviving the Ancient Faith*, particularly Chapter 10.

353  See *Pursuing the Pattern*, and various articles in *Truth Magazine* (February 2020), reporting on such discussions.

354  To cite merely one such example, consider an entire 2006 lectureship featuring "mainstream" preachers explaining "Why Anti-ism is Sinful" while trying to explain how "Opposing Support for Colleges from the Church Treasury is Not Anti-ism" or negating the question "Are We Holding a Form of Anti-ism Because we Oppose False Doctrine and False Teachers in ACU, OCU, Harding U, FHU, Lipscomb U, and the like?" or "When we Oppose The Church of Christ Disaster Relief Agency?"—from the website http://www.churchesofchrist.com for the Houston-area 2006 Spring (TX) Contending for the Faith Lectureship, "Anti-ism: From God or Man" (February 26—March 2, 2006). Other features included knowingly conflating views renounced by most if not all "NI" preachers (such as the "Anti-Bible Classes Doctrine" and the "Anti-Located Preacher Doctrine") or broadly attributing to "NI" churches "The Hats and Hair Doctrine" and other extreme views on "Classes and Woman Teachers." Nor is this sort of militant "anti-anti-ism" limited to a single "mainstream" congregation. For earlier examples of such rhetoric, sample the articles in notes 7–10 and 14 of the preceding chapter..

355  See Steve Wolfgang, "10 Things to Know About Orphan-Hating Antis," *Truth Magazine*, February 2020. An earlier (1998) attempt to situate the "NI" churches on the current landscape is Ferrell Jenkins' lecture at Pepperdine University, "Please Don't Call Us Anti," available on his website at http://bibleworld.com/notanti.pdf. Mac Ice's blog has also featured some suggested readings for "Understanding Non-Institutional Churches of Christ: Some Suggestions for First Reads," at https://mcgarveyice.wordpress.com/ 2009/06/28/understanding-non-institutional-churches-of-christ-some-suggestions-for-first-reads/

use and those who do not want it can refrain. This attitude leaves the basic issue unresolved.³⁵⁶

Unresolved, indeed. Still, no resolution is possible without frank discussion. Continuing brotherly dialogue is welcome and the need for candid discourse remains—while recalling the warning of David Lipscomb about the nature of apostasies:

> Apostasies come and will come. They come where the cause is popular, where an ease-loving and popularity-seeking spirit prevails, and always manifest themselves among those who avoid controversy and discussion. To suppress discussion is to deprive truth of all its vantage ground."³⁵⁷

## Viewing the Past, Looking to the Future

As seen in prior chapters, the division of the 1890s produced a majority of churches which, a generation later, divided into what became the Christian Church/Disciples of Christ, distinct from the "independent" Christian Churches which formed the North American Christian Convention— thus producing two roughly equally-sized groups. Meanwhile, the non-instrumental ("anti") churches continued on a growth trajectory, absorbing some who left various churches across a spectrum of both instrumental groups.³⁵⁸ By the 1960s, with the advent of yet a third generation, each of these groups had achieved roughly numeric parity. Furthermore, some have detected the beginnings of what might be seen as the same pattern developing among a second or third generation among "NI" churches.

By that time, this "pattern" can be seen to replicate in many ways, as the non-instrumental churches which had grown throughout the 20th century, experienced their own division in the 1950s, shedding a minority of "anti" churches. A generation later, by the late-20th century, the "mainstream" churches suffered their own separation into "progressive" and "traditional" churches—not so different from the 1920s division, which separated the Disciples from the more "conservative" independent Christian Churches. And both those groups continued their alienation from the "antis," who, despite perpetual predictions of their demise, continued their own growth

---

356  Jack P. Lewis, "A Cappella Music in the Assembly," Harding University Graduate School of Religion Bulletin, 39:1, January 1998, 1–2.
357
358  In truth, as with many divisions, seeing the results as a blended spectrum of overlapping beliefs and loyalties, rather than a clear demarcation into distinct groups more like buckets, probably lends itself to a more accurate understanding of reality.

trajectory into the late 20th century.

Of course, there are numerous exceptions to this pattern, depending on geography, timing, and abundant other factors, and it is always dangerous to try to group together people who prefer to emphasize congregational autonomy, the right of individual conscience, and an extreme allergy to anything resembling denominational grouping or language.

But the general pattern is too obvious to ignore. Well into the 21st century, features of the divisions of both the 19th and 20th centuries which may allow some generalizations. In both, a controversy involving congregational practices (not limited to matters of individual conscience) which involved a significant majority (perhaps 80–90%) of churches shedding a distinct minority which objected to certain "innovative" practices (instrumental music, church support of human institutions, evangelistic arrangements, and the public role of women in worship). After several decades, a second generation in the majority or "mainstream" produces a significant division among those churches, with shrinkage and significant exodus in both groups. Meanwhile, the discarded minority continues its own growth trajectory, and eventually the three groups may achieve roughly equivalent size of perhaps one-third each of the overall group—before beginning the trans-generational process all over again.

Perhaps the clearest prophetic foresight of things to come, based upon past hard experience, was provided more than a half-century ago by historian David Edwin Harrell, Jr.:

> Finally, the old seed remains. The fertile idea of "restoration" is as challenging to those people who are of a mind to accept it as it ever was. I have no doubt that it retains the same extraordinary and expansive spiritual force which it has twice demonstrated in the recent history of this nation. I am just as certain that success will ever bring with it problems, tensions, and schisms. Before we finish the work, we can look forward to the struggle of the future. It may be the struggle of my old age, or it may be the struggle of my son or grandson — but if the Lord does not come, it will. It would be trite and anticlimactic to say "history repeats itself." Perhaps it would be proper simply to conclude: "there is nothing new under the sun."[359]

---

[359] David Edwin Harrell, Jr., *The Emergence of the Church of Christ Denomination* (*Gospel Guardian*, 1967). Appearing first serially, and re-published many times since, this work is probably most easily accessible presently as a download at http://thecobbsix.com/wp-content/uploads/2016/01/Emergence-of-the-Church-of-Christ-Denomination.pdf

www.ingramcontent.com/pod-product-compliance
Lightning Source LLC
Chambersburg PA
CBHW041925090426
42743CB00020B/3438